POLO

BY

J. MORAY BROWN.

ILLUSTRATED BY

CUTHBERT BRADLEY.

London:

VINTON & Co., Limited,

9, NEW BRIDGE STREET, E.C.

—

1895.

PREFACE.

In response to a suggestion made to him by many polo players, the late Mr. J. Moray Brown undertook the preparation of this book, and had completed the work a short time prior to his lamented death on December 3, 1894.

As will be seen, he did not attempt to give a history of polo, as he had already dealt fully with that topic elsewhere. His aim was to prove the popularity of the game, to show how widely it was played, to furnish hints and instructions to beginners, to trace the formation and progress of many of the principal Polo Clubs, and to gather together in a handy form the rules and other current information in reference to the game. Before the matter had been put in type the author died, and the proofs have been revised by Mrs. Moray Brown, his widow, to whom the thanks of the publishers are due. In a brief introductory note which he had written, Mr. Moray

Brown expressed the hope that "a perusal of these pages may prove of use to young players, and that by reminding veterans of incidents similar to those in which they themselves have taken part, they may not be without interest." It may be said further that the book will also help to keep green the memory of one who did much to develop the game, on which he was an able and fascinating writer, as well as a skilful player.

CONTENTS.

———

ILLUSTRATIONS.

Goal 8 yards wide.

200 yards

300 yards

300 yards

200 yards

Goal 8 yards wide.

POLO.

CHAPTER I.

THE POPULARITY OF POLO.

S polo popular? Is it a game that has "taken hold"? Such questions are often asked by those who do not understand or appreciate the game, but if these querists were to take the trouble to study it in its scientific aspect, and the effect that it has on a man as a man; nay, if they follow its past history and trace its gradual increase all over the world, the answer will come glibly enough in the affirmative. Of its origin, shrouded in the mists of antiquity, and its history up to within a score or more years ago, I do not propose here to dwell, for is it not written in the Badminton Library volume on " Riding "? But for those who are sceptical on the point of its present popularity, it may not be out of place if I advance a few proofs in favour of my assertion. That polo can never attain the popularity of racing, cricket or football I will allow, but the reasons are not far to seek. In the first place it is a game which scarcely admits of gambling or betting in connection with it, and secondly, it is one in which the masses cannot indulge. And yet let a polo match be played anywhere where the populace can view it *gratis*, or at a trifling cost, and there the people will assemble "in their thousands."

Now what makes them do this? Simply the love that is implanted in the hearts of most Englishmen of witnessing any contest in which horseflesh plays a conspicuous part, and also the love of seeing their fellow countrymen engaging in a game that calls forth all those qualities which have made Britons what they are. I would venture no modest wager that if a polo match were announced to take place in Hyde Park some Saturday afternoon in June, you would see a greater concourse than the efforts of any agitating orator has gathered together, or even England's "Only (Salvation Army) General" could accumulate. The crowds present at Hurlingham or Ranelagh when the Champion Cup, the Inter-Regimental Tournament, the County Cup, or other important matches are being played, bear sufficient testimony to the popularity of the game with the classes ; but if you would see how the masses appreciate it go to the Phœnix Park in Dublin any day when a good game is on. Go to the Liverpool, Edinburgh, Barton-under-Needwood, or to the Elvaston grounds on similar occasions, and you will then see how the British public, little or nothing though they may collectively know of polo, appreciate it, whilst in India the European and native population are equally enthusiastic. To take one instance —Dublin to wit. We will say a match in the All-Ireland Polo Tournament is set down to begin at 3.30 p.m. Some three-quarters of an hour previous to this you will

see an endless stream of spectators on their
way to the polo ground in the Phœnix Park
—coaches and cars, landaus and dog-carts,
gigs and polo-carts all convey their loads,
well and ill dressed, and before play begins
there will be some ten thousand of "all sorts
and conditions of men"—ay, and women
and children—collected in a serried mass four
and five deep round the arena of contest.
An orderly yet appreciative crowd it is, and
not requiring the aid of the police to keep
it within due bounds. Then, too, the most
ragged gossoon knows not only the players
but most of the ponies as well, and though
the remarks that emanate from the crowd
may not always be complimentary, they are
generally very much to the point. Let me
give an example of which I was a witness.
The Freebooters, captained by Mr. John
Watson, were playing a trial match against
a regiment quartered in Dublin. At one
point of the game Mr. Watson, who was
playing "back," was hotly pursued by some
of the opposing team, and with no comrades
near enough to aid him, his position seemed
perilous. Two ragged little urchins, aged

some nine and six years respectively, had crept through the crowd *ventre à terre* (literally), and were watching and criticising the game as best they could, lying flat on the ground and obtaining occasional glimpses of what was going on between the legs of the spectators in the front row. "Ah! look there now," quoth one as Mr. Watson dodged the ball by a skilful tap out of the reach of his nearest opponent, and then hit a telling "back-hander." "Faith," observed his comrade in dirt and rags, "John Watson and Fritz wad bate 'em all by thimselves." "Begorra, an' he would," replied the elder; and he was not far wrong, for the remark was apposite enough, and showed that the youthful critics had taken the measure of the great player and his famous pony truly enough. Impulsive and excitable as the Irishman is, and imbued with horsey tastes, one can well understand his admiration of the game; but even the phlegmatic Scotchman is also roused to enthusiasm at times in favour of polo, and year by year the Edinburgh polo ground becomes more thronged now that the game and its good qualities are better known, whilst even the rural population at Rugby and other places appreciate by loud hand-clapping a bold bit of play, a good stroke, or a daring run.

If we go further a-field than our own tight little islands and see how the game has gained in popularity, we have but to look abroad. In India—though this is perhaps not quite a fair instance, since it is the cradle of Polo—there are not only Polo Clubs in many regiments, but in most stations the military and civilian element both worship at Polo's shrine ; whilst the many tournaments in which both European and native teams take part show how popular the game is. Putting aside the Inter - Regimental Tournaments, both cavalry and infantry, held at Meerut, Umballa, and Lucknow, others are held at Calcutta, Madras, Allahabad, Bombay, Poona, Hyderabad, Quetta, Kohat, in Rajpootana, and in the Punjab, at all of which teams from different parts of India compete, whilst several native rajahs —as those of Kuch Behar, Pattiala, Dholepore, Jodhpore, and the Nawab-Vikar-ul-Oomra—have their own teams, whom they spare no expense in mounting. In proof of my assertion that polo *is* a popular game let me refer the reader to the list of Clubs in various parts of the world, given in a separate chapter further on.

Nearly every cavalry regiment, both in the British and Indian army, has its Polo Club, and in most places where more than one battery of artillery is quartered the gallant gunners support polo. It is therefore unnecessary to enumerate them. But, as it is generally supposed that only the mounted branches of the service play polo, it may be as well to note that the following infantry corps all have Clubs (in many cases they are double battalion regiments), and doubtless I have omitted several from the list. The following, however, are the most prominent polo-playing infantry regiments:———Coldstream Guards, Scots Guards, Berkshire Regiment, Rifle Brigade, Buffs (2), 5th Fusiliers, 7th Royal Fusiliers (2), 13th Light Infantry (2), 14th West Yorkshire, 18th Royal Irish, Enniskillen Fusiliers, Lancashire Fusiliers, 60th Rifles, 61st Regiment, 79th Cameron Highlanders, and 3rd Bengal Native Infantry.

To turn again to India, in which, as I said, nearly every station has its Club, it may be noted the Staff of the Viceroy and the Governor of Madras can both put representative teams into the field; whilst we find figuring in Indian polo matches such Clubs as the Calcutta, Bombay, Madras, Ootacamund, Poona, Mhow, Hyderabad, Unceremonials, Rangoon, &c.

Now for the Western Hemisphere. America can boast of several Clubs, such as the New York, Westchester, whilst in other places Polo Clubs are springing up annually. Even in Canada and the Far West, Calgary, High River, Macleod, Pincher Creek, and other places, have regular polo gatherings, which are increasing in popularity, and where the cowboys think playing polo is better fun than "cow punching."

Perhaps the greatest stride that polo has made anywhere is, however, in South America, where there is now quite an English colony. Some four or five years ago polo was unknown, but now there are no less than twenty-five Clubs.

Perhaps the most remarkable thing about the way polo has become popular in the Argentine is that the natives are developing a taste for the game, and, moreover, seem to promise well towards being players. The following extract from a capital little paper published in Buenos Ayres, called " River Plate Sport and Pastime," and edited by a thorough English sportsman and good polo-player, will prove interesting In describing a match that took place between a Las Lomas team and Petacas, in which the latter, with the exception of Mr. F. Kinchant, were all native *peones*, the writer says: " Many who came to scoff were rather surprised at the good form shown by the Argentines. There is no doubt that if well taught these men will make first-rate players, a noticeable feature in their play being their quickness in getting on the ball, and the admirable way in which they back one another up. No polo-player need ever despair of getting a game, however isolated his *estancia* may be ; he has only to pick his men from the *peones*, and he can always ensure having a good knock up. As makers of polo ponies the natives will prove invaluable, and with training (one of these men had only played a few times), I venture to predict that the Petacas team will become one of the strongest in the country." * In this match, which was severely contested and only won by Las Lomas by two goals to one, "cowpunching" play is said to have been noticeable by its absence, and, much to everyone's surprise, there was no roughness at any time. To Mr. Kinchant and his schooling of the team much of their success was no doubt due, but evidently the willingness and the ability to play exists amongst the Argentine population.

I think I have said enough to satisfy most people that the game is not only popular but is becoming more so every year. I will, therefore, only add that Paris, Cairo, Jamaica, Hong Kong, and South Africa, Malta, Gib-

---

* This prediction has since been verified, for in 1894 the Las Petecas team were only beaten by the crack Argentine Hurlingham team by 5 goals to 4 in the Championship Tournament of Argentine. —J. M. B.

raltar, New Zealand, Australia, and even far-
away Samoa, can all boast their Polo Clubs,
and that, travel the world over, wherever half
a dozen Englishmen with horsey proclivities
are gathered together and a piece of suitable
ground is available, there will a Polo Club
spring up and "flourish" like a green bay-
tree.

But, it may be asked, why is the game
popular? What makes it so? Why do
men spend money and risk life and limb
simply for the sake of knocking a ball about
from the top of a pony? To such querists
I would propound another question. What
makes hunting popular? what cricket, football, racquets, or any other manly sport or
pastime? Is it not because they bring to
the front the exercise of manhood's physical
powers and encourage that spirit of generous
rivalry which must benefit all those who take
part in such games? And if a further reason
be needed it may be supplied by just that
element of danger without which we are apt
to consider any sport or pastime tame, for
very true are Lindsay Gordon's lines :—

" No game was ever worth a rap
    For a rational man to play
  Into which no accident, no mishap,
    Could possibly find its way."

As such, polo as a game must always appeal to the manhood of our nation, and particularly to soldiers, bringing to the front as it does all the qualities of courage, endurance, the ability to give and take, added to the calmness and judgment necessary in those who follow the profession of arms.

Add to this, the scientific aspect of the game, the combined knowledge of strategy and tactics necessary in a team who would win laurels, and, as a last item, its antiquity as the very oldest of games, and is it surprising that its votaries, nay, that many others, sing its praises enthusiastically?

As a proof of the value of polo as a game for soldiers, I cannot refrain from quoting an extract from a speech recently made by Sir George Greaves at Poona, when he was the Bombay Commander-in-Chief. In alluding to polo Sir George said: "I do not wish you to think that I have passed from the playing stage into the talking stage of this lovely game. Thank goodness I feel quite as keen on playing now as I did twenty years ago. Gentlemen, Sir Frederick Roberts has just given us an Army Order* on Polo, and I think it speaks volumes for the game that it should have worked itself into Army Orders. I do not know of any other game having been so honoured. *But polo is now an essential part of our army education.* It teaches men to ride and to keep their heads whilst riding." Sir George's pregnant words need no comment, for he, in a single sentence, which I have taken the liberty to italicise, advanced an irresistible argument in favour of polo, which must carry far more weight than any words of mine ; but I would beg those who may be in favour of discouraging such an eminently military and manly game to read and ponder these lines of Lindsay Gordon's, which I have slightly altered to suit the case .—

> " And some for their country and their Queen
> Would fight, if the chance they had,
> Good sooth, 'twere a sorry world, I ween,
> If we all went galloping mad,

---

* The Order referred to was one enjoining officers to wear a strong and protective head-dress whilst playing polo

Yet if once we efface the joys of the *game*
From the land, and out-root the stud,
Good-bye to the Anglo-Saxon *name!*
Farewell to the Norman blood!"

Be it remembered that not only have some of our most gallant as well as most scientific soldiers been polo-players, but that they are so still, and that in the polo field they have acquired that training which has stood them in good stead in the sterner strife of war. Is not this a clinching argument in favour of the game? I think it is. But let reformers do their worst, polo and its champions who love to play on the green turf of Merry England or the arid *maidan* of Hindostan, on the sandy plain of Egypt or the "Marsa" of Malta, will live long in memory when those who have been its detractors are forgotten, and so *Floreat Polo!*

CHAPTER II.

STRATEGY, TACTICS, AND DANGER IN POLO.

UBLIC knowledge of polo is limited, nor do the public study the game in its scientific aspect, for to most people the main idea presented by a polo match consists of eight men mounted on ponies, knocking a ball about. Perhaps I cannot convey a better illustration of what I mean than by describing a little incident I once witnessed at Hurlingham. It was a lovely July Saturday, just before the Inter-Regimental Tournament, and a trial match was taking place between the Royal Dragoons, whose team included poor Arthur Mesham, who subsequently died from the effects of a fall whilst hunting in Cheshire, and a Hurlingham team. The pavilion roof was fairly

thronged, when a lady and her attendant
cavalier took seats beside me. Now, it was
only natural to suppose that those who come
to the pavilion side of the ground should take
some interest in the game and know something about it, and, moreover, that, though
lovely woman may be ignorant of its intricacies, the sterner sex should be more en-
lightened. Yet this was the conversation
that passed at my elbow.

She : " What have they got to do ? "

He : " Oh ! don'tcherknow—er—one side
knocks the ball *this* way, and the other knocks
it *that* way."

She : " Oh ! indeed !   But what are those
blue-and-white things stuck up at each end
of the ground ? "

He : " Those ?   Oh !—er- let me see.
Those—er—yes, those are the goal posts.
They have to hit the ball between them, you
know. It's awfully hot ; wouldn't you like
some tea ? The tea is awfully good here,
you know."

And then they prattled on, doubtless
enjoying themselves thoroughly, but, in fact,
almost as ignorant of what was going on

under their very noses as babes unborn. This is no exaggeration, and is a fair specimen of what the majority of the public know about polo. To them it conveys little beyond several men galloping about on ponies, and hitting a ball backwards and forwards. They know nothing of the actual science of the game, any more than half the men who go out hunting know of the science required to hunt a fox. To the latter such niceties as being able to distinguish when hounds are running "riot" or a "heel line," or to take scent into consideration is so much Greek. They see hounds running, and without pausing to think *what* they are running, or what sort of a scent there is, they ride, and—often spoil sport.

But I am running riot myself, so to polo let me hark back, and point out how strategy and tactics can be applied to the game. Both these may be broadly defined as using the best means in your power to outwit an adversary, and may be employed either collectively or individually—that is to say, by a team and by every individual member of it. There is more in this than is apparent to the

2

ordinary onlooker, for a team must know when to turn defence into attack, and its members must be ready at all times to seize and make the most of an opportunity, and, if necessity requires, disregard the set rules laid down for their individual play and places in the game.   Let it not be understood that I am advocating such a departure from the general principles that rule polo, but in the great game of war, victories have occasionally been won by following such a course. Risk there no doubt is in setting rules at defiance, but it is the man whose mind can grasp a situation and who knows *when* he can transgress with impunity that fortune will smile on.

Polo is—or ought to be—essentially a game of combination, and every member of a team should play not for himself but for his side, and be ready to sacrifice the chance of exhibiting personal skill for the good of his side.   But, it may be asked, where does the strategy come in? In a dozen ways. I would ask those who disbelieve me to watch the play of such men as Mr. John Watson, the Messrs. Peat, Mr. Frank Mildmay, Capt.

GALLOPING IN LOCKED PAIRS.

Lamont, 9th Lancers, Capt. Renton, 17th Lancers, Capt. Spicer, Royal Horse Guards, Capt Le Gallais, the Messrs. Miller, and many others. Watch such men as these, note how often they, to use a Gallicism, *se réculent pour mieux sauter*, how often they provoke an attack merely to repel it and exhaust their adversaries, and then say, if you can, that there is no strategy in polo.

And as to tactics? Ah! that opens up a very wide question, one that can hardly be dealt with now in minute detail. Let me take an instance, however, where, aided by a cool head—we will, of course, suppose the player is mounted on a well-trained pony—a strong arm, and a straight eye, a player can afford very material aid to his side. We will imagine that a No. 2 is bringing the ball along, with his No. 1 " nursing " the opposing " back " and having his adversary on *his* left. A No. 2 who disregarded strategy and tactics would hit the ball in *any* direction Not so one who has studied the game. Such a one would try and hit the ball so that it should go *to the right* of both friend and foe in front of him. And the reason is apparent enough. By so doing, he would enable his No. 1 to still keep the front clear for him by keeping off the " back," and even afford No. 1, if opportunity arose and the ball was near the goal, a chance of scoring. To do this naturally requires precision in hitting, but it requires something more, viz., a cool head, a knowledge of pace *and* tactics. Then when the players in front have an opportunity, they should place themselves in such a manner with regard to their opponents as . will give whoever is in possession of the ball a fairly clear field goalwards, though, of course, to gain any advantage by such a tactical movement, the man who is in posses-sion of the ball must play *to* his side, for naturally his adversaries will endeavour to defeat the manœuvre. Yet, be it remem-bered, if the striker of the ball can hit accurately he will be able, by the use of tac-tical skill, to materially benefit his side by placing the ball either to the left or right. In other words, he can by doing so dodge and foil his antagonists. Of course he must use his judgment in this matter, and neglect, if he can afford to do so, any hard and fast rules, bearing in mind that his adversary is the one obstacle to be got past *somehow*. How to do this cannot of course be formulated precisely, and circumstances alter cases, but as the " Red Book" lays down for the instruction of young officers, " The intelligent officer will be able to avail himself of any means at his command."   I may not have quoted the context exactly, for it is many years since that interesting volume was my hourly study.   Still I think I have given the sense of the paragraph.

Of course under ordinary circumstances the ball should be hit straight up and down the ground as much as possible, but there are instances when it is permissible to do otherwise and take the ball round.   We will suppose that the ponies of one side are tiring, whilst No. 2 of the opposing team is on a fast and fresh pony ; if he gets on to the ball, obviously it will pay better for him to take the ball round, particularly on a boarded ground, for he will force the enemy to gallop after him and still further exhaust their weary animals.   His No. 3 will then probably have cut across into the centre of the ground, and to him No. 2 should then pass the ball.

All this sounds very easy on paper, and some may say it is nothing but theory. Still I think if such sceptics were to watch narrowly the play of such able exponents of the game as Mr. F. B. Mildmay, Captain Jenner, Mr. James Peat, and other shining lights of the polo world, they would note that almost their every move and stroke in the game was influenced by a motive, and that there is a great deal more required in a man to be a good player than merely being able to ride and hit hard, though, of course, to rank high he must be able to do both these. A feigned attack, the putting a too attentive No. 1 " off-side " by his opposing " back," keeping places in the game, dropping back to take the place of a friend who has gone up into the game, seeing where a friend is, and passing the ball on to him ; all these demand the exercise of much strategical and tactical skill, and in fact there is scarcely any limit to the possibilities of the game, or the perfection to which it can be brought by those who give their minds to the subject.

I trust I have briefly demonstrated that polo is not the wild hurly-burly it is commonly supposed to be, but a game requiring thought, judgment, and self-control, besides physical strength and horsemanship; and as such, surely it is one which most befits a soldier, and therefore is worthy of every encouragement as a military game.

A few words, now, about the danger of polo. Happily, in this country, serious accidents have been comparatively few, whilst none that I can call to mind have terminated fatally. In India, however, the case is different, and within the last few years the death roll has been somewhat long; consequently a cry has been raised against the game on account of its danger, and some three years ago this argument was advanced in favour of stopping officers in the Army from playing. In India, the fatal accidents that have occurred may be attributed to two causes—viz., the hard ground, and the fact that men often play badly-bitted and imperfectly-trained ponies. Yet another cause has been assigned as a reason—viz., the increased size of ponies, and it has been urged that in the early days of polo men were content to ride small ponies. Let us look into these questions.

The hard ground certainly is an evil that cannot be got over, and it is a factor which must be faced in any Indian sport pursued on horseback; but precautions may be taken, and Lord Roberts, when Commander-in-Chief in India, issued an Army Order in which he strongly urged officers to wear a stout and protective head-dress when playing. That in some cases such a protection may be beneficial, just as a tall hat fulfils the purpose in the hunting-field at home, is indisputable; but it cannot always have the desired effect, *vide* the case of poor "Bay" Middleton. A tall hat did not then save the neck of one of the most brilliant horsemen of the age when galloping on the flat, for he met his death full twenty yards on the landing side of the last fence he jumped.

To continue our examination of the dangerous elements of the game. The greatest of these undoubtedly arises from playing improperly-trained and badly-bitted ponies, and, I might add, playing ponies in blinkers. At home, as a general rule, ponies are fairly well trained, and considerable attention is paid to their bitting. But abroad it is different. A youngster in India buys a likely-looking pony, hacks him about a bit, introduces him to a stick and ball for a couple of days, and forthwith takes him straight into a game. What is the result? The animal, who has never been hustled about amongst a number of other ponies, gets frightened, becomes unmanageable, and forthwith, in his blind terror, bangs into another pony. There is a smash, and then "Another Fatal Accident at Polo" heads a paragraph in the newspapers. Common-sense, if nothing else, should point to the fact that a pony, before he is fit to play in a game, should undergo weeks, nay, months, of quiet handling and training; his education should be gradual; he should be looked on as a child, and taught on the same principle, viz., by slowly giving him confidence, and imbuing his lessons with interest. He should on no account be hurried or rushed into a game, or he will never become trustworthy, and, until he has been practised for some time in company with three or four other ponies, he should not be subjected to the ordeal of having seven galloping round, in rear and alongside of him.

There have, indeed, been some few exceptions of a pony playing the first time of asking, such as Mr. John R. Walker's Syrian pony Sinbad, which he played in a match at Cairo within five minutes of purchasing him, and after the pony had just come in from a long desert march. The pony then played as perfectly as he does now; but such exceptions only prove the rule.

Whilst penning these lines, I received a letter from a correspondent at Port Elizabeth, in South Africa, who has sought my advice on some points connected with the game. I give this extract from his letter :—"In training ponies for the game, I surmise that, in England, you give them a thorough drilling in bending and twisting; whereas *we* rush them straight off into a game, and let them learn it as best they can. . . . But here we generally ride in racing-snaffles." Now, this is what too often occurs, and yet people expect to get good ponies, and that they should play without any education! You might as well expect a chimney-sweeper to navigate an ironclad, and yet the public fancy this is how polo is played, and wonder that accidents happen!

Blinkers are an abomination, and ought to be forbidden on the polo field. A pony wearing them cannot see sufficiently well to avoid the rush of an adversary, and being

DANGER OF BLINKERS AND BAD BITTING.

taken unawares is more liable to get knocked over. If blinkers have to be used on account of a pony being " ball-shy," the sooner his owner gets rid of him and relegates him to

the humbler tasks of hacking or harness the
better, for sooner or later they are both bound
to come to grief.

Bitting is a most important point, and one
which I fear has too little attention paid to it.
No matter for what work used, an improperly
bitted horse or pony does justice neither to
itself nor to its rider ; both are playing at
cross purposes, and the result is mutual irrita-
tion and discomfort, to say nothing of danger.
I have always contended that with very few
exceptions no polo pony should be played in
anything but a double bridle.   No matter
how light a mouth an animal may have, his
rider cannot, with a snaffle, possess the same
power of pulling him up suddenly as he has
with a double bridle or curb, and consequently
the risk of accident is immensely increased.
Some may affirm that their ponies will not
face a double bridle properly, and will not go
up to their bits.   This, I think, is merely a
question of *hands*, and though a few, a very
few, ponies may play in a snaffle, such as Mr.
John Watson's celebrated pony Fritz, yet
such ponies are very few in a thousand. Here
again common-sense should clinch the argu-

ment, for the greater control you possess over any motive force the more you will be able to bend that force to your will, and, in the case of horseflesh, a suitable bit is the controlling force.

The increased size of ponies is one of the many causes to which fatal polo accidents have been attributed, and though, of course, I may be mistaken in my ideas on this subject, I cannot subscribe to the doctrine. It has been urged that when men played on 13 to 13-2 hand ponies no fatal accidents occurred. But how about one of the earliest victims to polo, poor Captain Clayton of the 9th Lancers, who was killed at Delhi on Christmas Eve, 1877? and he, I believe, was riding a 13-2 hand pony at the time. Then it must be remembered that the whole game has altered very materially of late years. Slow, dribbling play, with an occasional scrimmage, has given place to a scientific, galloping, hard-hitting game, in which a big man on a small pony would be nowhere. So, with altered conditions, bigger and stronger ponies had to be used, animals able not only to gallop faster but stand hustling without coming down.

Personally, I do not believe that the size of ponies has anything to do with accidents, except, of course, in the case of a small pony coming in contact with a big one, when the weaker is bound to go to the wall, or rather to the ground. But even if two ponies of the same size collide, one or both may fall, and there is still the chance of one rider being killed. If a small pony crosses his legs, cannons against another, or from any other cause comes down, he is just as likely to give his rider a fatal fall as a larger animal. The distance a man has to fall has nothing to do with the proportionate amount of injury he is likely to receive in that fall. If it had, would men ride 16-2 horses with hounds? Would they not prefer 15-2 animals as diminishing the risk of injury from a fall? A 14 to 14-2 hand pony—and now-a-days most ponies are nearer the latter than the former height—will not only carry his rider safer at polo, but his weight in a hustling bout is bound to tell. Besides—and this especially in the case of a long-legged man—he balances his rider's weight better, and does his work with greater ease both to his rider and himself. It has been urged by some champions of small ponies that they turn quicker and are more handy. This I consider a fallacy, and I would ask those who differ from me to note such ponies as Mr. John Watson's Fritz ; the Messrs. Peat's Dynamite, Gay Lad, Firefly, Grasshopper ; Lord Harrington's The Girl and Ali Baba ; Mr. T. S. Kennedy's Umpire and Dancing Girl, Capt. Daly's Wig, and many others, who have to carry big and heavy men. If they will do this, they will, I think, agree with me that many big ponies— mind, all these ponies are 14 hands, if not over—can turn like hares.

That all dangerous contingencies in connection with polo cannot be guarded against, no one will deny ; but much can be done, and the salient preventive measures I have endeavoured to sketch briefly. But before concluding my remarks on this subject I would draw the attention of polo players at home to the following resolutions passed at a meeting held at Poona, on March 11, 1892, and presided over by Sir George Greaves, then Commander-in-Chief in Bombay, who is a well-known enthusiast about all matters connected with polo. On this occasion the following resolutions were passed :—

1. That in view of recent accidents, and in order to keep the manly game of polo going, it is necessary for the players to take some steps among themselves to re-establish it in the favour of the authorities and the public.

2 That it is desirable to have umpires when practicable in ordinary station games, to enforce the rules, not only with a view to the safety of the players, but to train them, and to give them a full knowledge of the rules and to bring home to them the consequences of reckless play both in regard to its danger and its inutility in a match.

3. That every encouragement should be given to young players, but that every endeavour should be made to prevent men who cannot ride well enough, or who play unbroken or dangerous ponies from joining in the game.

4. That hustling should be discouraged as much as possible when neither player is actually riding for the ball.

5. That umpires should enforce the rules against unfair or dangerous riding without waiting to be appealed to.

6. That the present height of ponies should not be interfered with.

7. That subsidiary goals should not be introduced.

The first five of these rules are obviously so much to the point that I think they will meet with universal approval, and Nos. 4 and 5 are specially worthy of notice. Hustling is no doubt carried to absurd lengths, and I have seen two men, both first-class players, hustling each other at Hurlingham, when the ball was a good two hundred yards away from them, and play going on in a different part of the ground ; whilst in India the practice assumed I believe ridiculous proportions until very stringent rules with reference to it were framed by the Indian Polo Association. And with regard to No. 5, the subject is worthy of the consideration of the Hurlingham Polo Committee. Umpires should have every latitude given them, and *should be empowered to interfere without waiting to be appealed to.**

But here I am treading on delicate ground, and discussing a subject which I never intended alluding to. The ethics of polo might indeed furnish matter for a large volume, and so the sooner I practise what I have been preaching, and ride my pen in a curb, the better. A genuine love of the game must be my excuse for transgressing, but it *is* a grand game — one worthy of an abler

---

* This has now been done.—J. M. B.

scribe to bring its advantages home to the public. What I cannot do in prose has, however, been accomplished by that good sportsman, Mr. "Harry" Bentley, whose pen seems to glide over paper with the ease that his good horses cross the stiff country of Northamptonshire. Let me therefore borrow from him, and quote the following lines :—

"So search the world all over, take the pastimes,
　　one and all,
　　No better game than polo you can find ;
For, like life, its twists and turnings teach us all to
　　give and take,
　　And strengthen both the muscle and the mind
So the flying ball we'll follow ever on from goal to
　　goal,
　　Till minutes into hours swiftly pass ;
And we vow no other pleasure in excitement can
　　compare
　　To such a glorious gallop on the grass."

True words, these, and in years to come may there be many a good gallop on the sound turf of merry England, on the sun-baked *maidans* of Hindustan, in France, in Australia, America, and Africa, or wherever polo finds a home. So, *Vive le polo !*

CHAPTER III.

LETTERS TO YOUNG POLO PLAYERS.

I.

Y DEAR A——,

You tell me you intend to take to polo during the coming season, and ask my advice on certain matters connected with the "Royal Game." This I shall be delighted to give you, but first let me congratulate you on your determination to become a polo player. Depend upon it, you will not regret doing so, for it will not only teach you to become a horseman, but will considerably benefit you in other ways, particularly as you will —during your stay in London—be a young man "about town." I am not going to read you a lecture on how you should comport

yourself whilst enjoying your London season,
but would impress on you that if you mean
to shine as a polo player, you must not
"burn the candle at both ends," for if you
do, you will find your nerve fail, and that
you will neither be able to ride nor hit the
ball.

There are several points on which you will
need enlightenment, and such advice as I can
give is very much at your service, but I will
ask you to remember that no advice that I,
or anyone else, can give you will be much
good unless you make up your mind to practise self-denial in a great many ways, and go
in for the game with all your heart. You
may, no doubt, think when you look on at a
good game played by good men on good
ponies, that it is all very easy ; but you will
find, once you begin to try and hit a ball
about, or ride an imperfectly-trained pony,
that it is quite a different thing to what you
imagined, and that before you can even aspire
to play in moderate company you will have
to learn and practise many things, and until
you can do two things, viz., manage your
pony and hit the ball, I pray you not to

make an exhibition of yourself by playing in public. The points I shall submit for your consideration will not be many, but they will be important, viz., sticks, the choice and training of a pony, how to play the game, &c. ; but as I do not want to disgust you with too long a lecture, I shall not let this letter run to undue length. You will have some time before the regular season begins, and during that time, by constant practice, you will be able to do much towards perfecting yourself and your pony. I shall therefore select as the subject of this letter the sort of animal you should purchase, and if you are not able to find one already trained—which would be your wisest course—you will derive much pleasure in training him. Still, as teaching requires knowledge on the part of the preceptor, I should advise your deferring this until you have gained some practical experience.

You will probably have heard polo described as expensive and dangerous. Perhaps it is, as much as hunting or shooting, you will have to spend some money on it, for you cannot get really well-shaped, fast ponies without paying for them, nor can you go about playing matches or play in town at Hurlingham or Ranelagh for nothing; still, there is no need why you should pay an exorbitant price for your amusement. If you want to hunt in the Shires or take a grouse moor in Scotland, you will have to pay far more than you would if you are content to hunt with your country pack, and enjoy such moderate sport with a gun as your paternal acres will afford. In fact, you must cut your cloth according to your means, but if you will eschew tickets to theatres, giving dinners and supper parties, and other means of getting rid of your money, and expend your superfluous cash on polo, believe me you will be the gainer, both physically and morally.

Now, with regard to the dangers of polo, do not let yourself be influenced by the argument that it is such a very dangerous game. Certain elements of danger it undoubtedly possesses—and what sport worth a rap has not?—but not more than attend hunting, steeple-chasing, shooting, or even football, and such danger as there is, can be reduced to a minimum by the men themselves, if they play the game as it should be played, and ride properly-trained ponies.

You will want to know the sort of pony you should buy, and what his qualifications should be. You will probably not be able to get a perfect pony at first, but I will briefly sketch out for you what he ought to be like, and when you see one answering the description, take my advice and buy him. He or she—and many of the best polo ponies are mares—should have a clean, well-bred head, a broad forehead and intelligent eye, a well-set-on-neck, strong, flat legs, and good sound feet. The nearer perfection you can get shoulders the better, for though sloping shoulders are not absolutely necessary for turning quickly or for speed, yet good shoulders will often enable your pony to recover himself if he makes a mistake or gets knocked out of his stride. The pony's back should be short and muscular, the ribs well arched, and the loins strong; the quarters should be strong, long, and muscular, with length from hip to hock, and the second thighs well developed. Do not

despise a pony with a tendency to sickle hocks
or with a slight goose rump ; these points
may offend the eye as far as symmetry is
concerned, but an animal thus made, though
he may lose in speed from the conformation, can invariably turn quickly. Let your
pony show as much substance as a weight-
carrying hunter, the quality of a race horse,
and measure from 14 to 14.1 hands. With
the present uncertainty as to height, I cannot
conscientiously advise your buying one
over that height, though half the ponies
played, and some whose names are bye-
words in the polo world, are a good 14
hands 2 in. Personally, I think a pony
of the latter height the most desirable,
and though people will tell you that a pony
measuring a hand less is more handy, and
turns quicker, I do not believe it, and if you
go to Hurlingham and watch many of the
well-known big ponies, you will note that
they can turn and twist like eels. Besides,
a 14.1 hands or 14.2 hands pony not only
balances his rider's weight better, but, from
being heavier, is more able to withstand any
shock from being bumped into—as will hap-

pen at times—and so is less liable to come down You, I know, are not a very heavy weight, and a pony of 14 hands should suit all your requirements ; but see before you buy him that he has a good mouth, for a pulling, yawing, or boring brute, that wants a 20-acre field to turn him in, is utterly useless for polo, and will prove not only a source of misery to yourself, but one of danger to your friends. Ponies as well as horses go well in all shapes, and some of the best have not been the best-looking ; but, presuming that your purchase satisfies you on this point, and gives promise of being possessed of a fair turn of speed, it will be as well for you to consider what the qualifications are that are necessary to make him a good polo pony.

Briefly, they may be thus summed up, and I quote from such a good authority as Captain Hayes :—

1 He should be able to start quickly, jump into his bridle at once, and strike off from the halt into a canter or gallop.

2. His mouth should be so "made" that he will go at any rate of speed you desire,

from the slowest canter to the fastest gallop
—in fact, if he can " passage " at the former
it will be all the better.

3. He should be able to pull up to a
halt in a very few strides when at his greatest
speed.

4. He should be able to change his lead-
ing leg the moment he gets a hint to do so.

All these he can be taught to do in a
military riding-school, and if you have
neither the time nor the ability to teach him
yourself, you cannot do better than send him
to one, for they are the most important rudiments of his profession. When he has
learnt them, and been taught to give to your
hand and heel, you may proceed further with
his education. However, this will be a
matter for future consideration, and as you
will want to learn a good deal yourself, you
will require a handy animal at first. Do not
think it necessary to get a fast pony for your
initial lessons ; buy one that is thoroughly
trained, even though it may be a bit of a
screw. Arab, Barb, and Syrian ponies have
not only as a rule good mouths, but seem to
take to the game naturally, and so many of

these have been lately imported that you
should find no difficulty in suiting yourself,
and it will pay you far better to give a little
more for such a pony, than buy an English
or Irish pony which, though probably faster,
has not been well trained. South American
ponies, too, are wonderfully handy, and if
you do not object to their looks, and get a
well-broken one, you will find it of service.
Presuming you have got a suitable pony,
make it your business to discover in what bit
he goes best. This is an important point, to
which you should pay attention. And let
me strongly urge you to eschew a plain
snaffle, and use a double bridle, which, whilst
not irritating your pony's mouth or being
unduly severe, gives you command of him.

Your next step will be to learn to sit him
properly. You will probably be indignant at
my suggesting such a thing to you, but sitting
a pony when he turns sharply, as he will have
to do at polo, and when your attention is
concentrated on the ball, is a very different
thing to sitting a horse over a fence. You
will have not only to acquire grip, but learn
to balance yourself, and *not* hold on by the

reins. Begin by cantering your pony, giving him a hint when to turn by leg pressure and the sway of your body, as well as by a light touch of his mouth. Turn first to one side and then to the other, taking a serpentine course. When you find you have learnt the art of communicating your wishes to the pony without pulling and hauling at his mouth, make your half turns sharper and closer together, and then try a circle; begin with a wide one and gradually decrease it. After having done this you can practise getting your pony to turn right round when going at a hard canter, and then do it at a gallop. This will teach you a good deal, but you will perhaps learn more how to sit if you will adopt Capt. Hayes' method, viz., by getting someone to drive your pony with long reins and turn and twist him about whilst you sit on his back without any reins in your hand. This will teach you not to rely on reins as a means of keeping on your pony's back, and give you the confidence acquired by balance. Balance is a very important point in all riding, and the man who keeps his balance, and thus distributes his weight equally on a horse's back, affords the animal great assistance. In polo you have frequently to lean over considerably on one side, and if your pony is turning sharply at the time your loss of proper balance communicates itself to him, and the result will be that he is more liable to come down, as you, from your position, are unable to assist him in keeping on his legs.

Practise these few things every day for an hour or so until you feel perfectly firm in your saddle, and then try hitting the ball. The first time you endeavour to do this, and for many succeeding times, you will most likely miss it altogether, or not hit it fair. Some men will tell you to begin by going fast at the ball and to try hitting it at full speed, maintaining that unless you do so you are apt to potter over your strokes. Their opinion is entitled to respect, and may be correct, but on the principle that you must learn to walk before you can run, I contend that you should first learn to hit the ball fair and square at a stand, then at a trot and a canter, until your arm and eye so work together, that you can strike it accurately at speed. Learn to hold your stick properly, viz., at full length, not letting any part of the handle project beyond the level of your hand's palm. You will constantly see drawings in which players are depicted with a good three or four inches of their stick-handles visible beyond their hands. This is wrong ; for if you held your stick thus, the swing of the forward motion in a drive would, on the rebound consequent on the head of the stick meeting the ball, bring the projecting part of the former against your wrist, and so not only give you a nasty jar, but deprive the blow to be administered to the ball of half its force. Try the experiment yourself, and you will at once grasp my meaning. Hold your stick firmly, yet allow your wrist plenty of play, and avoid those abominations, leather straps attached to the ends of polo sticks. They are supposed to prevent your losing your stick ; they certainly fulfil this object, and also another, viz., that if by any means your stick gets caught you cannot release your hold of it, and are liable to be dragged off your pony. Cut off these

' HIT THE BALL WHEN IT IS IN A LINE WITH PONY'S FORE LEGS '

ERNEST BRADLEY

straps, therefore, and if you must have something to help you to retain your grasp of the stick, tie on a loop of thin tape sufficiently long to wind round your wrist, and of sufficient weakness that it will easily snap on any great strain being put upon it.

Begin by hitting the ball slowly at a walk; you cannot do better than try dribbling it a few yards at a time. This will be useful to you at times, for though the game now is one of hard hitting, there are times when a judicious dribble of a few yards to dodge the ball out of the way of an adversary, or to place it in a position for yourself to deliver a more telling stroke, will be very useful When you have mastered this, you can go on to hit harder and at an increased rate of speed ; and when going fast remember that you should hit *at* the ball *when it is in a line with your pony's fore-leg*, and *not when it is under your own foot*. This is the cause why balls are so often missed or not fairly hit Take the opportunity of watching Mr. James Peat or other hard and accurate hitters, and you will find that this is half the secret of their success

You will also have to practise back-handed strokes delivered on each side of your pony, as well as near-side forward strokes, and, moreover, go on practising until you have thoroughly established a thorough unison between your hand and eye When you have attained to a certain amount of efficiency, and can hit the ball fairly well when it is stationary, have one thrown towards you, or in to one side as it is at the commencement of a game. This will teach you to be quick *on it.* Meeting a ball is often necessary in a game, though it is a risky form of play ; but if you can hit it thus with a tolerable amount of certainty, you will be of great use to your team.

There is nothing more I can tell you that will ensure your perfecting yourself in the matter of striking the ball. The attainment of perfection in this matter can only be the outcome of constant and persevering practice, and it will depend mainly on yourself how proficient you become.

I have now allotted you a task sufficient for a month, and you will find that it will take you all that, and more, before you are

HITTING ON THE NEAR SIDE

satisfied with yourself. You will probably be disappointed that you do not "come to it" sooner, but do not be discouraged. Remember that Rome was not built in a day ; go on hammering away, and when you can report yourself as fairly competent to sit your pony properly, and hit the ball, I will give you some more hints, and tell you how to set about training your pony.

II.

Having in my last letter told you something of the stamp of pony you should try and suit yourself with, and how you should practise and train yourself, I now propose giving you some suggestions as to how you should train your pony (supposing that you have bought an untrained one), as well as on other matters.

First of all, let me give you a hint which you will find useful. Do not attempt to play in a very small saddle. You are not like James Pigg, of immortal memory, "lang and leet." The curves of your figure are graceful and symmetrical, and though I do not intend for a moment to hint that you are tending towards obesity, yet good living is apt to develop flesh and those curves which, to an artistic eye, are lines of beauty. Do not, therefore, lay yourself open to the charge— as I once did when riding a race many years ago in a 2 lb. saddle—of attempting to put "a round of beef on a cheese-plate"! When playing polo, as well as when hunting, you will have every muscle of your nether man called into play in order to retain your seat; you will often have, as assailant in a hustle, to lean right over your pony, and as a defendant you will have to do all you know to remain in your saddle; you will often, too, have to turn very sharply and balance yourself the while. You cannot do all these unless you have a good foundation or basis of operation, and that basis is a saddle which, without being clumsy, fits your pony well and gives you something comfortable to sit upon. You will find a surcingle a useful addition to keep your saddle in its place and prevent it from slipping.

If possible, avoid using spurs, but if you must have them, use blunt rowels. You are a smart man, I know, and a boot does not

look dressy without spurs, so if you must
have them, have the rowels taken out and
substitute sixpences. Your vanity will be
satisfied, and I am sure your pony will be.
About spurs, here is another tip : Have the
buckles removed, and let the straps that
come across the instep *button* on like the
underneath strap. Buckles are responsible
for half the cases of men being dragged
when they fall, for they catch against the
stirrup irons. " Looks so bad!" I hear you
say. Not a bit. Believe me, not one man
out of fifty will notice the change, and, after
all, which is of the greater importance,
appearance or life? You will be wise if you
sacrifice a little of the former for the sake of
ensuring safety to the latter.

One other bit of advice, and then we will
get on to the ponies, and that is as to a
head-dress. You know that in India, when
there was so much fuss, and absurd fuss,
made about the dangers of polo, Lord
Roberts, the late Commander-in-Chief, was
very strong on this point, and his remarks
were very apposite. Hunting hats are made
hard in order to break the force of a fall ;

and yet you constantly see men either playing polo without any covering at all to their
heads, or else with some wretched flimsy
thing made of silk. Now, swagger or in-
difference are all very well in their way, but
if a simple precaution may be the means of
saving your neck, why in the name of common sense not adopt it? The difficulty of
combining fashion with safety has, however,
been met, and by one of the best of our
polo players, Mr. Gerald Hardy. He has
invented a head-dress which combines a
certain amount of elegance with usefulness,
viz., a hard felt crowned cap covered with
loose cloth, which has all the appearance of
an ordinary cap—though *not* Mr. Keir
Hardie's pattern! I have ventured to call
this the " G.H.," which may stand for the
" Gerald Hardy " or the " Good Hat." And
you can get it at a hatter's in Jermyn Street
—the firm's name I forget, but if you make
a cast down the street you will find it. It
is, if I remember right, a corner shop.

Now for training your pony—and I am
presuming that you have paid me the compliment of carrying out the suggestions as

to yourself that I gave you in my last letter. You must start with the assumption that your pupil has everything to learn, and having discovered which bit he goes best in, you may commence his education. Do not, however, be in too great a hurry, or attempt to teach him too much in a short time. Education of every description, if it is to bear weight, must be gradual, and " cramming " is good for neither man nor beast. Your own experience will probably have taught you this ; apply it, therefore, to your pupil, and remember that the object you have in view is to teach your pony to obey your slightest hint from hand or leg pressure. What you have in view is to gain the mastery over him, and this can only be obtained by your keeping your own temper and—by perseverance. Once he knows that he *has to obey* you, *nolens volens*, you start with an advantage. You must work on his memory, and make him connect his education with kindness, though of course, like a human being of a low order, his feelings must occasionally be appealed to by punishment. The less of this you employ, how-

ever, the better. Bear in mind that you
have not only to educate him, but correct
his faults, and that nervousness is what you
will have to combat principally If you
succeed in removing the causes of this, you
will have gained half the battle. You may
have a stubborn pupil, you may have a
vicious one, but both can be subdued and
bent to your will, if you only take time and
—keep your temper. And, above all, do
not sicken and disgust your pupil with too
long lessons

One of the primary objects you have to
consider is to get your pony to carry his head
properly and go up to his bridle and yet
freely—I am presuming you have a pony
with a fairly well-set-on head and neck—for,
if he does not, he will not be much use as a
polo pony. You cannot do this better than
by fitting him with a standing martingale,
attached to *the rings of the snaffle, and not to
the nose band* as is so frequently done. This
will give you increased control over him, as
the mouthpiece will always remain on the bars
of the bit, and by preventing him from poking
out his nose, teach him that it is easier to

bend to the bit ; it will also make him move in more collected and more evenly-balanced form.   He will soon appreciate the relief, and this will be a point in your favour.   Having fixed your standing martingale at the necessary length, put on a driving pad, and with long reins passed through the pad terrets, drive your pupil about, first at a walk, then at a trot and a canter, making him the while turn to the right or left, pull up, or rein back.   But remember always that the reins must not be on his back.   For instance, if you want him to turn to the right, see that the right rein comes round his right quarter.   This will give you additional power and leverage.

You can do much, too, in speaking to him, and connecting what you want him to do with words.   Many will scoff at this, but you can prove the value of my advice by putting it to the test.   This practice with long reins on foot will make your pony attentive, teach him discipline, and give him confidence in his tutor.   It will repay you to give him plenty of practice with them, and you will by their use be able to overcome much of his natural timidity

Let me, therefore, strongly recommend
you to give your pony a couple of lessons
every day with the long reins, though, of
course, you should divide them into periods
of an hour, or an hour and a-half. Believe
me the time will not be wasted, and will considerably facilitate the furtherance of his education. If necessary you may help the pony
to carry his head properly by buckling reins
from his snaffle to rings on the roller pad,
when he is in his stall or loose-box; this may
be dispensed with except in the case of very
obstinate pupils, but its employment, as well
as that of the standing martingale, will teach
him to bend his neck to save his mouth.

I cannot undertake to teach you how to
acquire "hands," or that "magic touch"
which is the secret of horsemanship, but if
you will only bear in mind what a very delicate
organism a horse's mouth is, you may learn
much for yourself, and a *light* hand, remember,
will often control with apparent ease an
animal that "hangs" on his bit, pulls, or
fights with his head in the air when ridden
by a heavy-handed man.

When you have got your pony fairly

handy with the long reins, and properly
bitted, you may begin to ride him, and
pursue the course which I have advocated
in my chapters on Polo in the Badminton
volume on "Riding." It would be super-

~ EDUCATION IN BENDING OUTSIDE

fluous for me to repeat what I have said
there, and I feel that I cannot do better than
refer you to the book, only adding that
the " bending course " invented by Lord
Harrington is of the very greatest value.

Practise your pony well up and down this, circle about, and get him to turn to the right and left, pull up and turn quickly, and you will have advanced a very great step in his education.

EDUCATION IN BENDING. INSIDE

Now, a pony will do all this beautifully, but once you take a stick in your hand, and try to hit a ball off his back, you will frequently, and, in fact, generally, find that he is frightened. This arises from the natural timidity of the equine nature, and it will be your business to overcome it. It must not be done by harsh means, or you will connect the game with punishment in your pony's mind; you must, on the contrary, appeal to him by kindness, and demonstrate that his terror is unfounded. Before, therefore, you take a stick in your hand, or let him see a ball, let him understand that both are harmless; let him overcome his dread of them by constant association. You cannot arrive at this end better than by having a couple of sticks hung up in his loose-box, and by placing a ball there. If you watch you will probably note that he will sniff at them, push them about with his nose, and play with them; in fact, they will eventually become to him as toys, and he will disconnect them with all ideas of harm. When you go into his box to give him an apple or a carrot, take a stick with you, let him see it in your hand, and move it about in front of his head; repeat this when you get on his back, swinging the stick on each side of his head until he takes no notice of it. Then begin to hit the ball off his back, and

5

be as careful as possible not to let either ball
or stick hit his legs. You will thus overcome one great difficulty—viz., the tendency
most ponies have to shy off the ball, a very
aggravating fault, as you will find once you
have played on an animal who is addicted to
it. There is but one way of overcoming it,
and that is by imbuing the pony's mind with
confidence in you, and divesting him of the
idea that either ball or stick are going to
hurt him. They possibly may do so in the
future, but he will most likely then not
connect them with pain, and take matters
philosophically.

One point of importance I would call your
attention to, and that is teaching your pony
to meet other ponies; and with regard to
this, and the question of sore backs, I must
again refer you to the Badminton Library
volume on " Riding." Above all, do not
attempt to *play* your pony before he is fairly
well educated, and then only in a " cantering" game. If you do, he will get flurried
and alarmed, and half of the trouble you
have taken will have been thrown away.

About bits and bridles I have little to tell

you, but do not commit the mistake of playing in a snaffle. Some ponies will do so undoubtedly, but they are few and far between, and, besides, a double bridle gives you more control over your pony, it makes him go in more collected form, and turn on his haunches ; and this is what you want to make him do. Above all, never ride a pony in blinkers. They are an abomination and a very fruitful source of danger. If a pony will not play without them he is not fit for polo, and you had better relegate him to harness, or—pass him on to a friend. A whip you may at times find useful, and it is as well to carry one, for the best of ponies want rousing at times, and even if you do not use it in a game, it is as well to let your pony know that you have one in your hand, and that he is engaged in a more serious business than practice. Use it, however, with discretion.

What sort of a stick should you use? Well, that must depend on your own physical strength and the height of your pony. If you are not strong in your wrist, use a light stick. You will find the cigar-shaped heads

(Mr. John Watson's pattern) very handy, though I do not think they drive like the square-headed ones, and they are more likely to cut under the ball than heavier and squarer ones If you elect to use square heads see that the edges are bevelled off. A sharp edge may, if you miss your stroke, inflict an ugly cut on man or pony. The stick-heads are made of various woods—sycamore, beech, ash, willow, and birch, and in India, mango and seeshum are used; but you will find sycamore the best, it is light, durable and drives well The length of your stick must depend on the height of the pony you are riding, and should be of such a length that when mounted and grasping the end of the handle, your stick-head rests lightly on the ground. They are made in lengths varying from 4 ft. to 4 ft. 6 in., but the average length is about 4 ft. 4 in. The handles are made of ratan and malacca cane. The ratan ones are, I think, the best, for they are light, strong, and not so whippy as the brown malaccas. Avoid using a too whippy stick; you may not only suffer yourself—for instance, by the cane curling round when you try to hit a ball under your pony's neck and hitting *you*—but you may injure a rival bent on hustling you on the near side. Sticks will cost you about 5s. each, and you should keep at least a dozen by you, as you will need them of different lengths probably, and they often break just where the handle of the cane meets the stick-head, particularly in very dry weather. No very efficient remedy has as yet been discovered, though in India some men stand that part of the handle that fits into the head, in oil ; others soak their stick-heads and a few inches of handle in water or oil, but this naturally increases their weight, so you had better make up your mind not to mind sticks breaking. I would recommend you to use a flat-handled stick in preference to a round-handled one, for the former is less likely to turn in your hand at the moment of hitting. The former are considered the safest and best. From these suggestions you will, I trust, be able to suit yourself in the matter of sticks, and remember, what you have to guard against is having a stick which is too heavy for you. If your stick is unwieldy you will miss the ball frequently, though your eye may be true enough, and so you will be apt to become disgusted and fancy that you will never be able to play properly. If you want to know where to get sticks, I would recommend Salter of Aldershot, to whom most of the best men go.

You will do well to lay in a stock of balls. These are made of willow, and cost about 6s. 6d. a dozen, though if you purchase a "gross" you will get them cheaper. These can also be got from Salter.

Having now suited yourself with a pony and sticks, besides having trained yourself and pony, it will be time for you to study the tactics of the game, and learn how to comport yourself in any position you may be called upon to fulfil. In my next letter I will tell you the principles that should guide you when playing "No. 1," "No. 2," "No. 3," or when occupying the responsible position as "back." These, I trust, you will study and lay to heart, and if you do, we may some day see you a shining light in the polo world.

III.

This must be my last letter, and it will be devoted to telling you how to play the game. Before, however, offering you a few suggestions as to the main points you will have to study and bear in mind, when playing in different positions, I would invite your attention to one or two other considerations. Please do not think me a bore for doing so.

You must remember that every combination depends more or less on the units of which it is composed; and that a polo team is either strengthened or weakened according to the ability of its members to fulfil the duties of the various positions allotted to them, and to keep their places. No matter how brilliant individual members of a team may be, if they do not *play together* they will not make their mark. Reflect also on the fact that, in polo, strategy and tactics have to be considered in a very marked degree. Study these by precept and observation, and if you want a clearer definition I would refer you to what I have written in a former chapter. You will have to be greatly

guided by circumstances, to learn by experience when to be bold and when to be
wary ; to seize the right moment for turning
defence into attack, and make the most of
any weakness shown, or mistake committed
by your adversaries ; in fact, you will ever
have to be on the *qui vive* Let me recommend you to watch narrowly the play of
good men ; note what they do and endeavour
to imitate them. An ounce of practice is
worth a ton of theory ; and you will learn
more from observation than anyone can
teach you on paper. I would further impress upon you the absolute necessity of
keeping your temper and not losing your
head. The former will doubtless be often
tried, and the latter you will be frequently
tempted to do—under certain circumstances.
We will suppose, for instance, that you are
in possession of the ball, and that one of
your opponents, a wary veteran, tries to
"bluff" you, by shouting at you to "get out
of the way." Your natural diffidence may
lead you to fancy that you have no right to
be where you are. Visions of "crossing" or
being "offside" will flash through your brain,

and you will feel inclined to obey the mandate delivered, perhaps, in an imperious tone. You will get flurried, and your adversary having succeeded in putting you off—the very thing he is trying to do—will calmly take the ball from under your nose, and draw upon you the ridicule of foes and the anger of your own side. Be certain that you are right and then stick to it. Do not give way, for your adversary, when he sees that his little plan has failed, will be too wise to risk a collision, and you will probably have the satisfaction of having placed him in the predicament wherein he would fain have lodged you, and turned the tables on him. Study well the rules and definitions about "crossing" and "off-side." There may at times be excuses for transgressing the law of the latter, but for the former none. So, my dear A., resolve, whatever other faults or failings of which you as a polo player may be guilty, not to let the sin of "crossing"—which, remember, is *foul* play, productive of danger to yourself and your opponent, and for which a penalty is exacted —be laid to your charge. Polo is a scientific game nowadays, and rough and unmannerly play spoils it. It is quite possible to play with vigour, and to hustle without degenerating into "rough-and-tumble," and to preserve the instincts and courtesies of a man gently bred. No one yet was ever a worse soldier or a worse sportsman for being forbearing, and master of himself and his language under provocation ; and if, my young friend, you will carry out these principles, you will rise in your own estimation as well as in that of others.

Let me now have a talk with you as to what will be your duties as No. 1, No. 2, No. 3, and "back" respectively. Do not, I beg of you, make up your mind that you are more suited for one position than another. You ought, if you are to make a name for yourself, be able to play in *any place.* Granted, that after a while your particular capabilities may be more suited for one place than for another, still begin by learning to play in all. You constantly hear men saying, "Oh, I cannot play 'back,'" or "I never play No. 1 or No. 2," &c. Do not follow their example ; take cheerfully any place that may be allotted to you, and do your best in it; for if you can acquit yourself equally well in any position you will be a useful, even if you are not a brilliant player, and your services will be appreciated.

You will do well to begin by playing No. 1, and when so doing you must make up your mind that hitting the ball is to be somewhat of a secondary consideration, and that the main part of your duty is to harass your opposing "back" by every legitimate means; to thwart him and keep him off the ball on every possible occasion; and be a regular thorn in his side. Stick to him like a leech, and never leave him except on certain occasions when you have a clear field, and you see a good chance of hitting a goal. An uncontrollable desire to hit the ball is the great temptation every young player has to contend against, for we are all keen to have a smack at it, and earn distinction as goal-hitters. Some men cannot be made to understand and appreciate the harm they do to their side by not grasping the fact that, by keeping the field clear for their No. 2, they often are really doing more service to

their side than by striking the ball. I saw
an instance once in a match wherein I was
asked to coach some beginners. They all
vowed they would do what they were told ;
but once the game began, entreaty and
objurgation alike failed on my part to get a
certain " No. 1 " to stick to his " back." He
was a good horseman, well mounted, and
could hit the ball fairly well, but was so keen
on doing the latter that he neglected his
" back" entirely, and was always hanging
back and looking out for the chance of a
smack at the ball. I ventured to prophesy
that, unless he adopted different tactics, he
would never make a polo player, and the
only cure for him was to play for a while
without a stick. I fancy he did this, for
when I saw him play a year or two after he
had greatly improved.

Now, though your first and paramount
duty will be to keep your opposing " back"
off the ball, and to hustle him on every
possible occasion, you must not think that
you have nothing else to do ; but hustle at
the right moment only, and do not expend
your energies and those of your pony use-

lessly. Hit the ball occasionally you must, but you must watch your opportunity, and then quickly make the most of it, remembering that doing this must be made subordinate to taking care of your opposing " back," and keeping the field clear for your " No. 2." You must combine the two without carrying either to excess ; for the man who never hits the ball, and contents himself by "shadowing" his " back," is as useless in a team as one who neglects his " back," and thinks only of hitting the ball. You will constantly have to use your judgment, your observation, and your skill, altering your pace, judging your side of attack and defence, clearing the front for your " No. 2 " when your team is attacking, and, when defending, prevent your hostile " back " from coming up into the game. Circumstances alter cases , and, what may be a mistake under certain conditions, will be right under others. For these no mere theory can be advanced, and you will have to form your own judgment how to act. There is one thing you must guard against—viz., being put off-side by a " back," and to avoid this be careful not to get in front of him. A knowing "back" will frequently try to put you off-side by taking a pull at his pony, and letting you shoot past him, and so you must be careful to regulate your pace by his. I feel that I cannot do better than quote part of a letter written to me by Mr. John Watson, who is the finest all-round player the world has ever seen. He thus defines the duties of a "No. 1," after insisting that the latter, like every other member of the team, should be a good striker, and master of the ball :—" The two 'forwards,' No. 1 and No. 2, should work together, and, if possible, be exactly the same class of player ; but the least certain striker I should place as No. 1. His duty is to always keep one eye on the ball and the other on his opposing 'back,' always bearing in mind that it is his duty to prevent the latter getting the ball *just as much when the game is going against his (No. 1's) side as when it is attacking.* It is ridiculous to say that No. 1 should not strike the ball. He should invariably do so when he has an opportunity, unless he is shouted to by one of his side to 'leave it,' in which case he should pop the eye he has on the ball on to the goal, and keeping his other eye still on the 'back,' devote all his energy to get alongside his enemy, and *clear the road.* Should he manage to get up alongside, he should be careful not to let the 'back' drop away suddenly, and so put him off-side, but should hug him and hold him, as it were, with his knee. If the ball then comes in front of him, he cannot well tell what is going on behind. No. 3 of the other side should be up against his (No. 1's) 'second forward,' and unless shouted to 'leave it,' No. 1 should get the goal if he sees his chance. In fact, unless told by one of his own side to leave the ball, he should always strike. A team is weak if its No. 1 cannot strike ; but at the same time, a good rider, well mounted, may do grand service to his side by riding out the 'back,' and not striking often, yet not half so much as if he be a good striker as well. No. 1 should be very careful to know exactly when he is off-side, and, if even at all doubtful, he should not give the opposite side a chance of claiming a foul."

There you have the whole matter in a

nutshell, and only experience can teach you the right thing to do at the right moment, when to take the ball on and when to leave it ; but you must practise self-denial, and one of the first lessons you must learn and lay to heart is to be unselfish, to play for your side, and not for your individual gratification. Master the art of sticking to your "back" first, however, and when you have thoroughly learnt this, it will be time for you to practise when to hit and when to leave the ball. I am talking to you as a beginner, remember, and therefore would impress on you the former necessary point. You will have at times to be prepared to change places with your "No. 2"; and you must be quick to see when occasion requires you to do this, but do not do so unless imperatively called on, for it is a difficult matter, and one for which, if you attempt it unasked, you will probably not be thanked.

As "No 2" you will have an easy place, and one that should suit a man who, like yourself, glories in the elixir of pace. As "No. 2" you will have to mainly lead the attack, for you will be essentially the fighting

man of your force, constantly engaged in
attack.   Unless you are a good striker, however, you will be little good as " No. 2," for

"RIDE HIM !"

next to the " back," more will depend on the
accuracy of your eye and the strength of
your arm than any other member of your

6

team. You will have to be sharp as a
needle, ever ready to swoop down on the
ball and be off with it ; you must, too, keep
your wits about you every bit as much as
" No. 1," whose place you must be ready to
take the moment you see he is in possession
of the ball. Do not call to him to leave it
unless you feel confident about yourself, or
unless you see that the interests of your side
recommend such a course ; be ever ready to
play into your " No. 1's " hands, and, when
hitting the ball, note on which side of his
opposing " back " he is. I would lay stress
on this latter point, for it is one which is
very much neglected, and one in which the
value of *accurate* hitting is proved. Now,
we will suppose that you are embarked in all
the thrilling delights of a run ; that your
pony is going a good pace, and that your
" No. 1 " is doing his duty to perfection ; is
riding off the opposing " back " ; and is on
the *right* side of the latter. In such a case
you should—supposing always that you are
going in a direct line for goal—hit the ball
to the *right* of your " No. 1." His task of
keeping the " back " off will then be greatly

facilitated, whilst if he gets a chance at goal himself the odds in favour of his success will be increased by his having the ball on his right side. If, however, your "No 1" is on the left of the "back," hit to the left —in fact, hit the ball to that side which will best enable your "first forward" to keep the road clear for you. You should play to the player on your side, and this applies equally well when you are "passing" the ball, and do not hit it anywhere, and then expect your "No. 1" to ride off his adversary. If you make a point of doing this always whenever practicable, you will considerably lighten the duties of your "No. 1," for he will know on which side of him the ball is going to be hit without looking back, and so will manœuvre the "back" out of the way. Many men consider that as long as they hit the ball to the front, somewhere in the direction of their adversary's goal, they have done sufficient, but this, you will see, is not nearly so advantageous as hitting in one particular direction, and with a particular strength. Endeavour, therefore, to hit the ball to a place from which your forward player can keep his

adversary and so give you a clearer field.
This naturally reads very much more easy
of accomplishment on paper than it is in
reality, and you will doubtless experience
much difficulty in perfecting yourself. To
achieve a system you must persevere with
it and practise. Nor need you be discouraged if success does not crown your efforts
at once; but, believe me, when you have
attained proficiency in the particular point to
which I refer, you will find it pay. As a
" No. 2 " you should of course hit straight up
and down the ground as a rule; but cases
will arise when, as in the great game of war,
you will find that turning the enemy's flank,
and taking the ball round, will be distinctly
to your advantage. This you will be able to
do very frequently if the ground be a boarded
one and you are mounted on a fast pony—I
need not tell you that a " No. 2 " should not
be on a slow one—when the efficacy of such
strategy will be very apparent to you. Of
course you must ride hard and hit hard; and
I think I may sum up the rest of your duties
by telling you that your enemy's " No. 3 "
is your special opponent, and that you should

always be ready to take on the ball whenever it has been hit out from behind your own back line.

As "No. 3," or "half-back," much will depend on you, but the position, though onerous, is yet a very pleasant one. Your chief duty will be to keep a sharp look-out on your opposing "No. 2," and ride him off the ball on every possible occasion. Besides this, you must be ever ready to protect your "back," and assist him to keep the ball away from dangerous proximity to his goal. You should also be ready at the slightest hint to drop back and take his place whenever he goes up into the game; and when not wanted for this purpose go to the assistance of your "forwards." In a sharp attack you may often afford material aid by doing this, and help to overpower opposition. You must be good at "back-handers," quick to note every turn and phase of the game, and be prepared to play the "general utility man"; ready to hustle, make a run, hit up to your "forwards," act as "back," and occupy in turn almost every position in which you can render assistance to your side.

When you can do all these you will be one of the most useful members of a team, and earn unbounded gratitude from your comrades.

" What can I do as 'back'?" Ah! my young friend, that opens up a very wide question. What you should do on every occasion it would be as impossible for me, or anybody else, to strictly define, as it would be to lay down any law by which a general should conduct a campaign. Certain axioms and principles you will have, like him, to be guided by, but on occasions you will have to set these at defiance, and judge whether some bold *coup de main*, even though attended with risk, will not, in the end, prove the most advantageous strategy. As " back" you will occupy the most responsible position in the game, for not only will the burden of defending your goal rest immediately on your shoulders, but you will have to exercise the qualities of a commander, and direct, more or less, the movement of your forces. You will have to encourage and censure; inspire your comrades with confidence, and urge them to the

fight. To you they will look for incitement
to further efforts when the game is against
them ; on you they will depend for that
cheery word of praise which, when bestowed
by a leader, always stimulates. Be lavish of
such praise if you like ; but when you have
to censure, let it, I pray, be bestowed in the
language of a gentleman, and let not hot
words or foul language escape your lips.
Fault can be found, and reproof administered
—ay, with stinging effect—if such be your
object, without putting yourself on a par with
the *hoi polloi* of Billingsgate, or forgetting
that you are a gentleman ; and, if you care
little what you say before men, bear in mind
that ladies are frequently present on polo
grounds, and let not foul language pollute
their ears.

Forgive me, my dear A., for reading you
this lecture. I do not pretend to be better
than my neighbours, and fear that I have
often sinned in the matter against which I
preach ; but complaints have, of late years,
been frequently made about the unusually
strong language used on polo grounds, and
that the game encourages the use of such

language is one of the charges laid against
polo by its detractors. As far, therefore, as
lies in your power, prove that the accusation
is groundless.

As a "back" you will have, so to speak,
to be the "intelligence department" of your
team, besides being its leader, its reserve,
and directly responsible for the defence of
your goal. Now, many men think that as
long as they stick near their goal they are
carrying out the duties of a "back." This is
a fatal error, for, if you are not near your
fighting line, you cannot control it, nor afford
aid at critical moments There will be times
when defence can be suddenly, and with
telling effect, turned into attack. This will
most frequently devolve on you, and you
must therefore keep as near to the game as
you can conveniently trust your pony; while
if you have a sharp and fast pony you can
go nearer to the game than if you only have
a slow one. Let your defensive strokes be
mainly given in the shape of back-handers.
When galloping back to defend your goal
you must hit thus if you want to save time,
and if the ball be in front of your goal hit it

to one side, and take it out of dangerous ground. You frequently see an inexperienced "back" hit a backhander straight into the face of the attacking force, and it is needless for me to point out to you the folly of such a proceeding. You will be called on to "hit out" when the ball is behind your back line—at least, this is the general rule—though personally I have always held the opinion that "No. 3" is the man to do this. However, let that pass. On such occasions be careful not to hit the ball in front of your own goal, but to one side; you may at times find it advantageous to follow up your hit out, and take the ball on, but, if you do, shout to your "No. 3" to drop back and take your place, which you should resume yourself as soon as convenient. Do not attempt to meet a ball when defending your goal, except as a desperate resource, for if you miss it you leave the road clear for the attacking force; it will be far better for you to turn your pony and wait for the chance of a back-hander. You must be prepared at times to come up into the game and lead the attack; but, before doing so, be certain that your " No 3 " is to be depended on— that he grasps the situation and takes your place. You will, of course, be considerably bothered by your opposing " No. 1," but you can also bother him to no slight extent by always trying to put him off-side, which can be done by letting him get between you and your goal. Watch Mr. John Watson, Mr Arthur Peat, or Capt. MacLaren, and you will see how this can be effected. Let your guiding principle be the steady defence of your goal, and sacrifice every other desire for great deeds to that object Much will depend on how you comport yourself at critical moments, and on your quickness and decision You must temper boldness with caution, be Argus-eyed, and frequently practise self-denial ; you will then possess the qualities of a leader, and inspire your team with confidence

Such are the main points that you must be guided by in your play in different positions. That you will prove yourself such an Admirable Crichton as to strictly observe them all, I doubt ; you will constantly fail, and commit many mistakes ; but you can at least try. Be not discouraged if you fail ;

time and practice work wonders, and if you persevere and carry out the spirit of the suggestions I have laid down for your guidance you will succeed. Let me advise you, once you have mastered the intricacies of the game, have a handy pony, and can hit the ball well, to play as much as possible in *good* company. Nothing will stimulate you more, nothing will afford you more practical experience, or demonstrate to you your weak points, than playing with men who understand their business. You will never discover your faults if you are content to play always with men of your own calibre, or possibly inferior to it. Then, when you have made a name for yourself, remember you too were once a duffer, so be lenient to the shortcomings of others, and when asked to play with inferior players, do not look glum and object. Be guided by what Lindsay Gordon says :—

> As far as you can, to every man
> Let your aid be freely given.

You will be respected for so doing, and do much towards advancing the interests of the glorious game.

I have now given you all the advice I am capable of imparting; and as you possess youth, courage, and a liking for the game,

RIDE HARD,

HIT HARD

DON'T LOSE YOUR TEMPER,

AND NEVER "CROSS"

I hope you may profit by what I have told you. Apply precept to practice, and where precept fails, let common sense and observation serve you. I have nothing more to add,

except this : Ride hard, hit hard, keep your
eyes open and your mouth shut ; stick to a
good pony when you have got one, and be
temperate in living ; do not lose your temper, and never "cross."   Then shall men
speak well of you, and in time you will
occupy a niche in the temple of polo fame.
So good luck to you.

Believe me, my dear A——,

Yours faithfully,

J. MORAY BROWN.

CHAPTER IV.

About some Provincial Polo Clubs.

I.

T is an acknowledged fact that the popularity of polo is yearly increasing, in spite of the sneers indulged in against it by some who should show a more generous and sympathetic spirit where horseflesh and a manly pastime are concerned ; and, as I do not wish to make an assertion that cannot be substantiated by facts, I take up my pen to give a brief account of some of the best known provincial Clubs With a few of these I am naturally fairly well acquainted, but not being endowed with the faculty of being everywhere, I have been obliged to depend on the kind courtesy of others with regard to the history of certain Clubs ; and so, without further preamble, and with grateful acknowledgment to those who have supplied me with information, let me come to the point, premising that I follow no table of precedence in seniority or in any other matter, but jot down my notes as the various Clubs recall themselves to my mind.

THE LIVERPOOL CLUB. — It was in the autumn of 1872, when polo was in its infancy, that the late Mr. Hugh Gladstone started the Royal game at Liverpool, and in those early days its devotees used to play on their hunters with long sticks. This was naturally found unadvisable, though judging from the increased height of ponies during the last few years, and the indecision of the Hurlingham Polo Committee about fixing polo pony height, we may before long find men reverting to the ancient practice! But this by the way. At any rate, twenty-two years ago the then most prominent members of the Club found it did not pay to play on horses, and bought ponies At that time none were keener than the Messrs. Heywood Jones, of Larkhill, including the popular

Captain "Wengey" and his brothers, "The Boss," Oliver, and "Bengey," better known, perhaps, by their sobriquets than by their surnames. Other supporters of the Club were Mr. Henry Stock, the Messrs. Gladstone (of Courthey), Mr. R. E. Graves, Mr. George Warren (better known as "Cock Warren"), and Mr. R. Haig, whilst the officers quartered at Liverpool also took no little interest in the game, and played at Childwall, where the Club still have their ground, some of them being included in a team that Liverpool sent to play at Lillie Bridge, when that place was looked on as the head-quarters of polo.

After an existence of a few years, however, the polo spirit waned; the Club became moribund, and, though the Messrs Heywood Jones and a few others kept the game alive at Larkhill, the Liverpool Polo Club became, for all practical purposes, extinct. In 1885, however, it rose, Phœnix-like, from its ashes, and to Mr. William Lee Pilkington, its present hon. secretary, it owes its *renaissance*, for it was his energy and sporting spirit that warmed up into a blaze the dying embers of the sport, conjured back the spirit of polo, and put the Club again on its legs. How this was done it may not be out of place to mention. The idea originated at a dinner given by Mr. George Lockett at the Liverpool Racquet Club, when the terms of a match between two ponies were being made and discussed. Mr. Lee Pilkington, seeing his opportunity, suggested that the Polo Club should be re-formed. Several of those present agreed to the proposal ; so, going on the principle of striking while the iron is hot, Mr. W. L. Gladstone produced pencil and paper, took down the names of those who aquiesced, and the existence of the Liverpool Club, which has ever since gone on and prospered exceedingly, was *un fait accompli.*

The Club at present consists of the fifty playing members, to which number the Club is limited, besides over 200 honorary members at a yearly subscription of one guinea each. The ground situate at Childwall is fairly level, but apt to get bumpy. It is boarded, and, like the Wirral ground, is formed in a way that might with advantage be imitated by other clubs, for *inside* the boards the turf is raised slightly, so as to slope upwards towards them ; so that the ball seldom if ever hangs, but rolls back, thus giving a man who is coming fast at it a good clear shot. The length of the ground is 255 yards, by 127 yards wide—rather narrow, perhaps, yet not to be grumbled at. There is a charming ladies' pavilion, now considerably enlarged, with tea-room, boudoir furnished with great taste, and balcony ; and also one for members, with dressing-rooms and refreshment bars This pavilion since my last visit, has, I hear, been considerably enlarged and raised, and possesses now the advantage of having seats on the roof, from which a capital view of games can be obtained. Attached to these buildings, and in prolongation of their line, there is an excellent range of stabling, while few, if any, provincial Clubs can boast such attention to the comforts of members and their friends as the Liverpool Club. Certainly none can have a more untiring, courteous, and energetic hon. sec than Mr. Lee Pilkington, who, being a keen poloist himself, has worked hard to rear an offspring that does him infinite credit.

Keen to foster polo spirit, the Liverpool Club not only annually send a team to compete for the County Cup at Hurlingham, which they won in 1891, but go so far afield as to do battle with the Edinburgh Club, which latter occasion is generally a very pleasant and festive one, the rivalry of the polo field being tempered with that *camaraderie* and good-fellowship which should always exist when the mimic strife is o'er. Gathered haphazard, I may mention the following as some of the most prominent members of a Club which often turns out nearly forty members of an afternoon, all keen to have a smack at the ball:—Mr. W. H. Walker, Messrs W. Lee and G. H. Pilkington, Mr. A. Tyrer, Mr. C. E. Mason, Mr. "Tannar" Graves, Messrs. J. and D. Irvine, Messrs. A. T. and H. C. Neilson, Mr. Munro Walker, Mr. George Warren, Mr. S. M. Dennis, Mr. H. Miller, Mr. F. Tinsley, Messrs. W. W. and H. Kellock, Mr. George Lockett, Mr. T. H. Stock, Sir Peter Walker, Mr. C. Nicholson, Mr.

Stollerfoht, Mr. Hodge, Mr. J. Bateson, Mr. Edmonson, and Mr. Burgham. The Club colours are chocolate and pink.

THE WEST ESSEX POLO CLUB was started in 1878 at Epping by Messrs. A. Waters, G. H. Dawson, H. B. Yerburgh, and B. Dickinson, of whom the first three still remain members of the Club. Polo was then only in the stage of "short frocks" in England, and the Club, which played upon "The Plain," a common lying between the town of Epping and the Lower Forest, was carried on in a rough-and-ready fashion for a couple of years, the matches being confined to one or two against the Bishop Stortford and Cambridge University Clubs

In 1880 Major Tait became the hon. secretary of the Club, a post which he still holds; and, thanks to his energy, the Club was regularly organised, with a list of nineteen members, of whom nine still belong to it. In 1882 Mr. Chisenhale Marsh, of Gaynes Park, near Epping, came to live at home, and at great expense enlarged his cricket ground in the park into the present polo ground, which he has ever since generously placed at the disposal of the Club. This ground is now one of the best in England, being 300 yards long by 200 wide, and consists of sound old turf, surrounded by trees, and with a beautiful view across Gaynes Park and the valley beneath, towards the high ground of Epping Forest It is not boarded, and is given over for the use of the Club by Mr. Marsh rent free, the only expense the Club has to bear being the keeping it in order and the necessary attendance. This enables the Club to do with a very moderate subscription. On obtaining the use of so good a ground, the members increased to about thirty, all living within a radius of about eight miles from Epping, of whom about half are now playing members. Among the most prominent of these have been Mr. Waters, a very hard hitter, who is Captain of the Club; Mr Dawson, who unfortunately has for some years been unable to ride owing to an injury to his hip, received in a polo match at Bishop Stortford ; Mr. Chisenhale Marsh (a most energetic No. 1), Mr. Alfred Suart, Mr. Alfred Kemp, Mr. Sydney Kemp, Mr.

Sheffield Neave, Mr. Walter Buckmaster, and Mr Robert Ball. The last was, perhaps, the best player the Club has produced, and his death in 1890 has been a loss which it has never recovered.

During its existence the Club has played matches with varied success against Cambridge University, the 13th Hussars, the 12th Lancers, and other regiments quartered at Colchester ; the Royal Artillery, Hertfordshire, Kent, Ashstead, the Dagenham Priory, Stansted, and other clubs, and has several times competed in the County Cup Tournament at Hurlingham. There, however, it has met with but little success, owing to its members being outclassed in ponies by its rivals, although it has at different times won matches against every one of the Clubs above mentioned.

One of the most interesting contests in which the Club has taken part was an annual tournament instituted by Colonel Studdy, R H A., between the R.A. Club, Woolwich, the Hertfordshire Club, and the West Essex. This continued for several years, and the cup was held by each of the three Clubs in succession ; but, on the breaking up of the Hertfordshire Club, in a final contest for the cup between the R.A. and the West Essex, it was won by the former, who now retain it.

As the Gaynes Park ground is within a mile and a-half of Epping, where good stabling can be had, and to which there is a good train service, it might be well worth the while of players from London, who find Hurlingham and Ranelagh too crowded to get as much play as they wish, to join the West Essex Club. Men go as far to play golf ; why not do so for polo ? The hon. sec., Major Tait, Epping, will give any information wished on this subject, and those who want a good gallop over sound turf, good polo, and a hearty welcome might go further and fare worse.

THE WIRRAL CLUB was inaugurated by Mr. G. K. Catto, hon. sec., and Mr. F. W. Blain, the hon. treasurer, in 1885, at the same time that the Liverpool Club was re-started, as before mentioned. For the last eight years, however, Mr. F. W. Blain has ably filled both posts. When the Club was first founded, the principal players were

Messrs. C. M. Nicholson, H. Nicholson, R. Haig, A. Hassell, G. Ravenscroft, G. K. Catto, and F. W. Blain. More recently other well-known names have been added to the roll, such as Messrs Ravenscroft, A. H. Wrigley, A. D. Chambers, F. C. Dale, F. Wignall, W. A Ball, and F. Tinsley. The ground is situated four miles from Birkenhead, and one mile from Spital Station. Its area is about seventeen acres, the actual playing-ground being 250 yards long and 180 yards wide ; it is boarded. It might, indeed, be more level in some places, but the ground is sound old turf, with thick herbage, and though, from being on the clay, it is apt to crack in very dry weather, yet under ordinary circumstances it plays well. Like the Liverpool ground, it is made to slope slightly up to the boards There is a commodious pavilion and shelter stalls for about twenty ponies. The playing days are Wednesdays and Saturdays, but the ground is open every day for practice. There are a good number of members, but those who may really be called playing members do not, as a rule, exceed about a dozen. With

the exception of the Liverpool Club, there
are but few in the neighbourhood, but
matches are played with the various regiments stationed within reach, and the Liverpool and Manchester Clubs, and with
Edinburgh, whilst the newly-formed Chester Club, started by Mr. A. Tyrer, will add
to the number. The Wirral men, however,
are imbued with one very necessary element
to success, they are all keen, and love the
game, and though circumstances do not
permit of their mounting themselves as well
as they might wish, they have all studied the
game, play good sound polo, *and gallop*.
We shall, I trust, hear more of them in the
future, and one day see them win the Blue
Riband of county polo. They should certainly have a try for it, judging from what
I have seen of their play; and, should they
win, their success will, I can assure them, be
warmly applauded as that of true sportsmen.
Their colours are yellow and black.

THE EDINBURGH CLUB.—Twenty years
ago, when the 7th Hussars, in which H.R.H.
the Duke of Connaught was serving as
a Major, and my own regiment, the 79th

Highlanders, constituted the garrison at
Edinburgh, polo was in existence in the
North, and once or twice a week play used
to take place in a field near Duddingstone.
Those were the old days of small ponies, the
dribbling game, and charging for the ball;
and I remember with a shudder even now
a collision which took place between His
Royal Highness and myself, how in the
charge we met—I will freely acknowledge
that the fault was mine—how we both went
heels over head, and how I thanked God
that my Sovereign's son experienced no ill
effects from my awkwardness. I can picture
the whole scene—my Royal opponent's strug-
gling white pony and my own wretched
"tat" mixed up on the ground, and the
generous and kindly words of reassurance
as we rose and I faltered out a breathless
apology. But how changed is the story
now, for the Edinburgh Club at present
ranks high amongst provincial Clubs, and last
year won that coveted trophy, the County
Cup at Hurlingham.

In a desultory way the game was kept
going till 1888, when Mr. T. B. Drybrough

took the matter vigorously in hand, and then the Edinburgh Club began to be heard of. About seventeen acres of land at Murray-field, situate only a mile and a-half from Princes Street, was rented, and a ground laid out which has the advantage of scenic surroundings, it being backed by the Murray-field Woods, from which several snug and picturesque villas peep out. The soil below the surface is gravel and sand; this causes it to dry rapidly after rain, of which they have more than their fair share in the North, and so it always rides light. The length of the ground is 300 yards, and from goal-posts to goal-posts 260 yards, whilst the width is 175 yards The ground is a boarded one, and there are besides an ample lawn and pavilion, surrounded by a broad verandah; a good hall, dressing-rooms, kitchen, &c. There are stalls for thirty-two ponies, a band stand, a large wooden shed for tea and refreshments, two lawn tennis courts, public and members' lawns, an archery ground, and an open military menège 120 yards long by 20 yards wide, which is a most useful adjunct for schooling ponies in.

The Club is in a most flourishing condition, and at present, I believe, numbers nearly 500 members, of which some five-and-twenty play with fair regularity, whilst that most sporting and polo-loving corps, the 12th Lancers, now quartered at Edinburgh, supports the Club as loyally as did their predecessors, the 4th and 13th Hussars, to whose initiative, coupled with Mr. T. D. Drybrough's (the hon. secretary) energy and keenness, Northern polo owes much. The matches at Edinburgh are mainly confined to games with civilian members and the military; but once every year Liverpool and Wirral send teams to the North, whilst Edinburgh also goes South to meet them. For the last two seasons Edinburgh has sent a team to compete for the County Cup at Hurlingham, and won it on both occasions. The most prominent civilian members of the Club are Messrs. T. B. and W. J. Drybrough, Messrs W and G. Younger, Messrs. James, John, and Charles Craig, Mr. H. B. Towse, Mr. T. W. Tod, Mr. W. D. Gibb, Mr. R. Usher, and Mr. Connal. The Club colours are black and white.

THE LUDLOW CLUB. — Started in 1892, this Club owes its origin to the initiative of Mr. W. Howard and Mr. T. McMicking, has as its President Lord Windsor, and numbers about thirty-five members. The ground, which is a small one, and not boarded, is most picturesquely situate at Bromfield, inside the Ludlow Racecourse. Play takes place twice a week from May till August, when a Gymkhana meeting winds up the season. The most prominent players are Messrs. Boyd, H. Cunninghame, A. E. Gerard, F. R. Hill (hon. sec. and treasurer), Hugo H. Martin, T. McMicking, J. H. James - Moore, and E Tredennick, and, though the Club is too young to venture far afield in search of glory, there is a growing keenness amongst its members which augurs well for its future success. The Club colours are light blue, black and yellow.

THE MANCHESTER CLUB can trace its origin as far back as most other Clubs, for it was founded in 1872 by Messrs. Colin Ross, Ashton Radcliffe, Bailey Worthington, and others. For five years it flourished fairly well, and then died. In 1881, however, the

cavalry regiment then quartered at Manchester—to which regiment the honour be-
longs I have failed to ascertain—began to
play, and their example was continued by
the Queen's Bays, who have of late years so
distinguished themselves on Indian polo
fields, till 1884, when they left. Their
example bore good fruit; the civilian element recognised the advantages of the game,
and Messrs. James E. Platt, Walter Roberts,
and Septimus Lambert founded the present
Club, which, however, suffers much from
want of local players, and is mainly dependent on the cavalry regiment quartered at
Manchester. The ground, which is full-sized
and boarded, is, on the whole, fairly level
and well turfed. It is situated at Old Trafford, about three miles from the centre of
Manchester. A pavilion and shed are attached, and play generally takes place three
or four days a week. Sir Humphrey de
Trafford is President of the Club, Mr. Fritz
Reiss, Vice-President, and the committee
consists of Messrs. C S. Lyon, L. Carlisle,
F. Tinsley, R. L. Cranshaw, and W. J. H.
Jones, with Mr. Percy Hargreaves as hon.

treasurer, and Mr. Douglas Phillips hon. sec. The Club colours are chocolate and yellow.

THE BOWDEN CLUB.—This modest and comparatively little - known Cheshire club may justly boast of an earlier origin than any, for it was originated in the early "sixties" by Messrs. Gaddum and Symons, who had come home from India bitten with the charms of the game. They went at it with a will; sent to Exmoor for a consign- ment of ponies, and got a ground at Cheadle, a suburb of Manchester. Their well-meant efforts, however, bore but little fruit; most of the ponies died; and, as far as I can gather, only one game was played. Mr Gaddum's health soon after broke down; the Club died out and was not revived till 1891, and I think I am right in stating that it owes its present existence to its hon. sec., Mr. Harry E. Gaddum, a nephew of the original founder. The Club at present con- tains about thirteen playing members, mostly business men at Manchester, but these can generally be relied on to play regularly dur- ing the season. On Mondays and Thursdays members are able to get a gallop at 6 p.m.;

on Saturdays the ground is open at 3 p.m., and it is very rarely that owing to weather or want of players a game is not played. The ground is a poor one, not very level, and only 220 yards long; there is a shed for ponies, whilst a tent is pitched for tea and refreshments. Most of the players can boast of one pony apiece only; but, by avoiding matches and letting every member feel confident of getting a game whenever he turns up, they manage to get a great deal of enjoyment, and put in sixty days' polo, more or less, from April to August.

I think the example of the Bowden Club, unpretentious as it is, is worthy of imitation All men cannot afford to keep several ponies or to play high-class of polo, but most men can afford to keep one mount, learn to hit the ball, and acquire the rudiments of one of the most entrancing of games. By keeping down expenses within reasonable limits there are few counties or large towns where a Club could not be formed on similar lines, and such a scheme, if formulated widely, would not only do much to increase the popularity of polo, and do away with the idea that it is *de facto* an expensive game, but would also encourage pony-breeding, and give many people that essential object for healthy exercise during the summer which is so necessary for hard-worked business men. It is to be hoped that in many districts the good example set so unostentatiously by the Bowden Club will be followed, for it is as possible to enjoy polo without any very ruinous expense as to enjoy hunting, shooting, or fishing in moderation.

THE WELLINGTON CLUB is the latest recruit to the ranks of polo Clubs, and was started in 1894 by Mr. A. C. C. Kenyon-Fuller, in conquence of the Staff College Club being given up, and the military authorities very foolishly prohibiting polo at the Royal Military College, Sandhurst. At present there are only about twelve playing members, most of whom live in the neighbourhood; but soldiers at Aldershot help the young Club, and Reading should also be able to furnish a contingent to keep the game alive. The ground, which I hear is a very fair one, is situate close to Wellington College Station, on the S E.R ; capital stabling can be obtained at the Wel-

8

lington College Hotel ; whilst the subscription
(£1) is so small that it should attract many
beginners who are keen to learn the rudiments
of the game in the seclusion of the country.
As an old Wellingtonian myself, I must confess to feeling much interest in this Club, and
trust that being able to run down and watch
polo may have a beneficial effect on the rising
generations of schoolboys at the school which
bears such an honoured name, imbue them
with its charms, and so result in the old school
turning out many a poloist as brilliant as
Capt. Malcolm Little, of the 9th Lancers.
The Committee of the Wellington Club consists of the Hon. R. W. Ward, the Hons. O.
and R. Molyneux, Capt. Jeaves, and Mr. A.
C. C. Kenyon-Fuller (of Finchampstead,
Wokingham, Berks, who acts as hon. sec.),
and the ground is open for play on Mondays,
Wednesdays, and Fridays during the season.

THE STANSTED CLUB is an instance of how
keenness for the game, though confined
within a limited area, can be developed, for
this Club was only really started very late in
the autumn of 1892. There was hardly time
then to do more than lay its foundation, lease

a field, and get a few players together, but Mr. Tresham Gilbey inspired others with a fondness for polo, and the outcome was the present Club. At the time mentioned I was paid the compliment of being asked to come and see them start. Few of the members knew much about the game. The ground was rough, full of rabbit holes, and on a slope, whilst ponies were none of the best. But the raw material was there, men anxious to learn, and not above doing so ; moreover, they galloped and rode hard, and if they did not always hit the ball, they did their best to keep their places. In 1893 they started with renewed energy, played against Cambridge and Rugby, and derived considerable benefit from the experiment, and last season, with true sporting spirit, entered for the County Cup at Hurlingham, and the strong Rugby team had all their work cut out to defeat them in the first ties. Their example is to be most warmly commended, for they exhibit that true *esprit de polo* which in the end is bound to succeed.

Since then a new and much improved ground has been made at Bishop Stortford.

It is 290 yards long by 130 yards wide, and, being well turfed, rides sound. It is boarded. There are eighteen playing members, of whom fifteen are nearly related to each other by the bonds of brotherhood or cousinship, and the Committee consists of Messrs. Herbert Blyth, Philip Gold, and Tresham Gilbey, the last named acting as hon secretary. Mr Walter Buckmaster, who has played with such *éclat* for Cambridge University for the last few seasons, is one of the Stansted Club's most prominent members, as is Capt. Breeks, R.A ; whilst two other members distinguished themselves in the rowing world, viz , Mr. Harcourt Gold, who was stroke for the Eton boat which won the Ladies' Plate at Henley last year, and Mr. W. F. C. Holland, who was President of the Oxford University Rowing Club, and rowed in the 'Varsity boat for two or three seasons.

The Club meets for practice on Tuesdays, Thursdays, and Saturdays Their colours are light blue and gold, and if they go on as they have begun they should have a bright future before them.

THE FETCHAM PARK CLUB.—In 1887 Mr

Walter Peake originated the Ashtead Polo Club, and, his father kindly giving the use of a field, play began in that year. For five years the Club prospered, and in 1890 played in the final tie for the County Cup at Hurlingham, on which occasion they were beaten by the Berkshire County Club, after a very tight game, by 2 goals to 1. In 1892, however, Mr. Peake left Ashstead, and the ground, always a small one, being no longer available, the Club migrated to Fetcham, where Mr. J. Barnard Hankey placed a ground in his park at their disposal. They then assumed the title of the Fetcham Park Polo Club, the constitution of the Club remaining unaltered.

Three hundred yards long, 180 yards wide, not boarded, and very level, the polo field is most picturesquely situated on rising ground, whence a lovely view is obtained, whilst it is backed by the magnificent timber of Fetcham Park. The turf is good, and, being full-sized, the ground affords ample scope for galloping, a privilege of which the playing members take full advantage. It is most conveniently situated, being only three-quarters of a mile from Leatherhead. There is stabling for thirty ponies, dressing rooms, and tea pavilion, and two stands for spectators, so that it may boast of being as complete as any provincial ground, and more so than most.

The Club consists of about 120 members, and though on first going to Fetcham Park they were rather short of players, they now muster about twenty who play regularly, the most prominent at present being Messrs. L. Paine, L. Cobham, T. Brandt, E. Courage, and J. Budd. The playing days are Monday, Wednesday, and Saturday, and the Club colours are red and grey (stripes).

Several matches are played during the season, and in 1894 a very successful handicap tournament was held, in which four teams competed. The Club has for the past few seasons sent a team to take part in the Abergavenny Tournament, and won the cup there in 1892.

Mr. J. Barnard Hankey is President of the Club, with Messrs. A. G. Moon, W. Fraser-Tytler, Ronald Peake, J. E. Budd, and T. E. Brandt as a committee, whilst

Mr. Ronald Peake acts as hon. treasurer, and Mr. Arthur G. Moon, Fetcham Rectory, Leatherhead, fulfils ably the position of hon. secretary,

THE RUGBY CLUB.—Within rifle-shot of the famous Hilmorton Gorse, and on ground famous in the annals of hunting, where the Pytchley, Atherstone, and North Warwickshire all converge to a central point, there sprang into existence some three years ago a Club which bids·fair to become the best in the provinces. Until the year 1891 Rugby had never been stirred by the polo spirit. Hounds and horses were its main attractions, and during the summer months its residents led a sleepy sort of existence till the advent of another hunting season roused them into activity, But all that is now changed, for Rugby now is as lively in the summer as it is in the winter, and this has been owing to the magician's wand waved by the Messrs. Miller, of Spring Hill, the founders of the Rugby Club. It may not be here out of place to trace how in a short time great results have been attained from small beginnings, and to show how the Club sprang into existence.

In 1891 Mr. George A. Miller and his
brother, Mr. E. D. Miller (who when serving
in the 17th Lancers played for his regiment
in several inter-regimental tournaments, both
in India and at home), bethought them of
combining business with pleasure, by training ponies and dealing in them. With this
object in view they cast about for some suitable spot, and found it in Spring Hill, the
farm of the late Mr. John Darby, the well-
known Rugby dealer, whose name must be
familiar to every hunting and horsey man.
The surroundings of Spring Hill—130 acres
of good grass land, with boxes and stalls
capable of accommodating fifty-seven horses
—were eminently suitable for the enterprise
the Messrs. Miller proposed embarking in ;
and, once settled there, they set about making
a polo and practice ground, and then starting
a Club. There were naturally difficulties at
first. Some residents looked askance at the
new scheme, and there was a dearth of
players in the immediate neighbourhood.
Energy and tact, however, soon overcame
all opposition ; the advantages of such a Club
became recognised ; men came to see, try,

and buy ponies, and found the ground so good, and the class of polo played so high, that they joined in numbers, and I think I may venture to assert without fear of contradiction that none who have ever bought a pony at Spring Hill, or played on its ground, have regretted doing either the one or the other. This by the way, however, for I would not pose as a puffer of ponies ; and, besides, Messrs. Miller's reputation stands too high to need such adventitious aid as any words from me could afford them. And so the Club, once having taken root, grew and flourished, a good number of playing members joined it, whilst it was not long before the neighbourhood testified their approval by subscribing liberally, till now there are over eighty members, of which thirty-six may be reckoned on to play with fair regularity.

The ground is 285 yards long by 175 yards wide, and formed out of a field of sound old ridge and furrow, now levelled as flat as a billiard table. It is boarded, and like the Liverpool and Wirral Clubs, the turf slopes upwards to the boards. There is a com-

modious and covered stand, besides a tea
and refreshment pavilion, and any amount of
stabling in the farm buildings adjoining the
ground, where ponies can be sheltered in
wet weather, whilst numerous benches afford
the good folk of Rugby resting places from
which they may watch the game and become
imbued with its charms.   The President of
the Club is the Earl of Denbigh, and the
Vice - President Mr. A. James.   Lieut.-
General Tower, Messrs. E. Chaplin, A.
Brocas Clay, R. Beech, N. Rhodes, G. A.
Miller, and Captain Beatty form the Committee, and the duties of hon. treasurer and
hon. secretary are ably filled by Messrs. A.
Brocas Clay and E. D. Miller respectively.

The Club colours are dark blue shirt and
light blue cap.   The playing days are generally Mondays, Wednesdays. and Saturdays,
and the Rugby Tournament, which was so
successfully inaugurated in 1893, is now
recognised as one of the events of the polo
season. The Rugby Club, both in 1893
and 1894, sent a team to compete in the
County Cup Tournament at Hurlingham,
and also to the Paris Tournament, as well

as to Abergavenny, and, though successful in none of those contests, gave a very good account of themselves, considering that they are such a young Club. Growing in favour and support day by day, they have a brilliant future before them ; and, being composed almost entirely of men who go well to hounds, they should earn the highest distinction, whilst the day is perhaps not far distant when we may hail the Rugby men, mounted on Spring Hill ponies, winners of the blue riband of polo, the Champion Cup at Hurlingham.

A word in conclusion, and this at the expense of appearing to vaunt other men's wares. The Messrs. Miller have now built a large riding school at Spring Hill, 90 ft. by 30 ft., and here their raw material, in the shape of ponies, is subjected to that careful and systematic training which few ponies get before they are allowed to see a stick or a ball. The advantages of such, and the being able to continue education regardless of weather, are obvious ; and to this thorough training the Messrs. Miller's ponies owe their well-deserved high character. But, whether he goes to buy ponies or to play polo, at any rate from the Rugby Club the stranger will meet with nothing but the most cordial welcome, play on one of the best of grounds, and meet some of the best of sportsmen.

I ought perhaps to mention that the most prominent playing members of the Club are the Messrs. E. D. and G. A. Miller, Mr. C. Beatty (so well-known as a gallant man to hounds and a steeplechase rider), Mr. R Beech, Messrs. A. and J. Belleville, Mr. Howard Cartland, Mr. W. F. Inge (Master of the Atherstone), Mr. T. Jameson, Mr. A. Jones, Mr. P. A. Leaf, Mr. H. J. Selwyn, the Earl of Shrewsbury and Talbot, Mr. W. A. Tilney (17th Lancers), Mr. A. Tree, Mr. John R Walker, Captain D. Daly, Mr. A. Burnaby, Mr. A. Batchelor, and the Earl of Craven, whilst frequent attendants are such well-known poloists as the Earl of Harrington, Mr. Gerald Hardy, and Mr. E. B. Sheppard.

THE WARWICKSHIRE CLUB.—Much senior to the Rugby Club, but its near and very good neighbour, is the Warwickshire Club, which has its head-quarters at Leamington, and was founded about 1884 by Messrs. F. Shaw, Albert Jones, and the late Major Green, to the initiation of which latter, I believe, the Club really owes its origin. Be that as it may, records show that on March 26, 1884, it was recognised that such a prominent place as Leamington should have a polo club ; so a meeting was held at the Tennis Court Club, and this was attended by Major Green, Captain Prior, Messrs. W. M. Low, Bond-Cabbell, Kingsley, E. Trepplin, Charrington, J. F. Shaw, the Hons. D. and S. Leigh, and C. W. Bell. There the subject of establishing a polo club was discussed, its establishment decided on, and games were played in Warwick Park and on the Racecourse. After the first flush of excitement, however, the game languished, and though the Club was never broken up, it did not meet with any very hearty support till 1887, when it took a new lease of life, and in the following year the present ground, on the Sydenham Farm, Radford Road, Leamington, was taken on lease and made. This is now all that can be desired, being perfectly level, capable of being watered, and measuring 268 yards long by 152 yards wide ; it is boarded, and like the Liverpool, Wirral, and Rugby Clubs, has the turf slightly raised inside the boards, and sloping to them. Watering a polo ground is always a matter of difficulty and expense, but the keenness and liberality of the members of the Warwickshire Club have overcome this obstacle, and arrangements have now been made for the ground being watered, so that it can be played on in even the driest weather. This is undoubtedly a great advantage, and one of which the Club may be justly proud. The ground is within easy reach—one mile, I believe, the correct distance—of the L. and N.W.R. and G.W.R. stations at Leamington, and stabling can be had in the immediate vicinity.

The Club numbers amongst its members eighteen who are non-players and twenty-one who play with fair regularity. Amongst the latter the most prominent are Messrs. A. Batchelor, C. Beatty, R. G. Beech, Howard Cartland, the Earl of Craven, A. C. Jones, P. A. Leaf, M. J. Selwyn, the Messrs. Miller (from Spring Hill), F. Shaw, Mr. A.

M. Tree, and Mr. H. Powell (Warwickshire Regiment). The hon. secretary is Mr. P. A. Leaf, and, the Warwickshire Club may now be looked upon as being in a most flourishing condition, and as one of the rising county clubs. Their colours are dark blue and French grey.

THE STAFFORDSHIRE CLUB. — Amongst county polo clubs of recent origin, perhaps the Staffordshire Club shares with the Wellington the position of being the youngest, and it may aptly be termed the offspring of the Earl of Shrewsbury and Talbot's sporting and enterprising spirit ; for, though in the early days of polo a Club existed which played at Lichfield and Stafford alternately, it never had a serious existence, and soon died out. It is only within the last two seasons that his lordship has regularly taken to polo, but, once he became bitten with its charms, he took to it *con amore*, purchased the best ponies that money could buy, and became a red-hot enthusiast. That he has attained no mean proficiency those who witnessed his play in the Paris and Rugby Tournaments as well as at Hurlingham in

1894 will readily admit, and now he has earned further polo laurels by establishing a Club and making a ground at his residence, Ingestre Hall. This was laid down two years ago, and, having been carefully tended ever since, will soon be in splendid condition. Distant four miles from Stafford and one mile from Hinxon Station, it is full-sized, well turfed, and very level. It is near the River Trent, from which Lord Shrewsbury has laid iron pipes all round the ground ; these are connected with hydrants ; with these and the aid of his private steam fire-engine, the ground can be thoroughly well watered. There is plenty of stabling at the Home Farm, within 200 yards of the ground, and the train service is excellent. The Club consists of twenty-five members, amongst whom may be mentioned such well-known names as the Earl of Harrington, Captains the Hon. R. Greville, Daly Fergusson, " Wengey " Jones, and Renton, Messrs. John Reid Walker, E. D. and G. A. Miller, N. T. Nickalls, Portal, Gerald Hardy, E. Selwyn, A. Burnaby, and A. Jones.

Mr. J. K. Bisgood is the honorary secretary, and the Club colours (which can be obtained from Messrs. Beale and Inman, New Bond Street) are :—First team, red and yellow ; second team, pale yellow and white.

THE CAMBRIDGE UNIVERSITY CLUB. — Founded in 1873 by the Hon. John Fitzwilliam, this Club may be said to have attained its' majority and turned out some of the most brilliant players of the day. Its records, too, have been kept with fair regularity for some ten years, judging from a book kindly placed at my disposal by Mr. F. B Mildmay, M.P. From this it appears that, though they used to play all the year round, it was not till 1878 that the game was seriously taken in hand, rules framed, and an inter-University match against Oxford decided upon. The colours of the Club were maroon and yellow, and, after some discussion, and with the sanction of the Cambridge University Boat Club, the following rule was passed :—" That the Polo Five (*i e.,* the five who ever have or shall play against Oxford) be allowed to wear a light blue polo shirt. white forage cap, and belt." To this there

9

is the following *addendum :—" N.B.*—Any-one playing for the team may wear the blue shirt for that game, but that game *only*, since he *must* play against Oxford to be entitled to his blue."

In 1878 the game was further encouraged by the Captain, Mr. W. E. C. Ellis, present-ing a medal die to the Club, to print silver medals for the trial fives, together with five silver medals for that year.

The first inter - University match was played on the Bullingdon Cricket Ground at Cowley (Oxford) on November 27, 1878, in pouring wet weather ; and as many of those who took part in it have since made names for themselves, it may not be unin-teresting if I copy from the book before me :—

Oxford.	Cambridge.
Miles (Capt)	W. E. C. Ellis (Capt.).
Stock.	R. A. Bayley.
Green-Price.	H. C. Bentley.
Kavanagh.	S. C. Mitchell.
Leigh.	H. R. Jameson.
Colours :	Colours :
Dark Blue.	Maroon and Yellow.

Umpires :

Story
C. A. Wood.

The game seems to have been protracted, and to have lasted an hour and a-half, at the end of which Oxford won by 5 goals to love.

The following year we find Cambridge competing for the Champion Open Cup at Hurlingham, but they were defeated by the Wanderers in the first ties by 3 goals to love The same year they turned the tables against Oxford, when they played at Hurlingham, and defeated them by 2 goals to 1.

In the meantime the game increased in popularity, and many members joined the Club, but in 1880 Oxford were victorious, and won by 4 goals to 1, though in 1882 Cambridge won by 3 goals to love. In 1883 the match seems to have been a hard-fought one, ending in a draw with the score 1 goal all. Four days after a return match was played to decide who should be the winners, and on this occasion Cambridge won by 3 goals to 2.

The era of playing four men a side instead of five then dawned, and the next time Cambridge met Oxford the former do not seem to have distinguished themselves, from the following comment accompanying a description of the match :—

" In this match, as in all previous University matches, the Cambridge men were all abroad during the first part, and seemed to quite lose their heads. During the second half, however, they had considerably the best of it ; but luck was against them, and they were unable to score." The final result was that Oxford won by four goals to love.

Here my information comes to an end. Between this match and 1889 (when I first saw the inter-'Varsity match) no one seems able to tell me how often either University won. In 1889 Cambridge won by 7 goals to love. In 1890, after a hard fought game, each side being 4 goals all at the end of time, Oxford eventually hit the goal that gave them the victory by 5 goals to 4 ; and in 1891 Oxford were again victorious by 4 goals to 1. In 1892 Cambridge put such a strong team together—the best ever sent by them to Hurlingham—and consisting of Messrs. G. Heseltine, W. C. Harrild, W. S. Buckmaster, and L. MacCreery, that Oxford had no chance, and were defeated by 12 goals to 1 ; whilst in 1893 they were again victorious by 6 goals to 1, and besides, made a very good fight for the County Cup, being only beaten in the semi-final tie by Edinburgh, who eventually won the cup by 1 goal.

So much for past history, but, from all I hear, they have no youngsters coming on, and the game at Cambridge seems to have passed its zenith.

The ground at Cambridge is a good one, and full-sized, but boarded down one side only. It is situated one and a-half miles from the town, and play takes place on Tuesdays, Thursdays and Saturdays during the Summer Term. Mr. W. S. Buckmaster is the hon. secretary.

THE OXFORD UNIVERSITY CLUB.—It is with regret that I can give but scant information about this club, which, I believe, was started in 1874 by Mr. Walter Long, who has since distinguished himself so much in the political world, and who brought some friends up from Wiltshire, and commenced operations in a cut hay-field. The Club records seem not to have been regularly kept, though this may to a great extent be owing to the Club completely changing

every two or three years, and this enhances
the difficulty of obtaining information regard-
ing its early history. Still, that the game
has been kept alive at Alma Mater is evi-
denced by the information I have given in
the accounts of the inter-University matches,
when Oxford seems to have had its fair
share of successes.

The Oxford ground, which is 280 yards
long by 170 yards wide, and not boarded, is
in Port Meadow; but as this is near the
river, and subject to being flooded, play takes
place during the winter on the Bullingdon
Club ground. The number of playing members seems to average about a dozen, and
the playing days are Mondays, Wednesdays,
and Fridays. Since 1889 the following have
been captains and hon. secs., the duties being
combined :—1889, Mr. N. C. Cockburn;
1890 and 1891, Mr. K. Pulteney; 1892, Mr.
A. Dugdale, 1893, Mr. G. N. E. Baring;
whilst the position was in 1894 filled by
Viscount Villiers, New College, Oxford.

THE SWINDON CLUB.—Though conducted
on modest principles, and never going far
afield in search of glory, this Club is another

instance of how men anxious to have healthy exercise during the summer can do so by playing polo. Who its originator was seems shrouded in mystery, and, though it was started some fifteen years ago, it had for the first years of its existence rather a chequered career, being— owing to members leaving the neighbourhood—constantly broken up and then re-formed. The present Club was started four years ago, mainly, I believe, owing to the encouragement given it by Major T. C. P. Calley, 1st Life Guards, who lent them a ground at Burderop Park ; and, by taking part in games himself, and bringing a regimental team down to play, gave an impetus to the game. The present ground is the Wiltshire County Ground. It is very small, and far too narrow, being only 220 yards long by 80 yards. Yet within this limited area its members get plenty of fun and generally disport themselves on Tuesdays and Fridays. The surface is old turf, taken up in 1893 and relaid in 1894 after being levelled, so that the ball travels very true. The Club consists of fifteen members, of which some ten, including Dr. McLean, the Messrs. Deacon, Mr. Lawrence, and Dr. Toomer, of Fair View, Swindon, who is the hon. sec., are the most regular players.

THE CHESTER COUNTY CLUB is the revival of one which was started in 1881 by Lord Arthur Grosvenor, Mr. J. Henry Stock, M.P., Messrs. Ashton, C. Shaw, A. D. Chambers, A. Hassall, J. Knowles, C. Lane, and W. H. Walker, and owes its resuscitation mainly to the efforts of Mr. A. Tyrer, a well-known member of the Liverpool Club, and a most enthusiastic poloist. In former days the Club used to play with fair regularity, though it was not till Lord Harrington, who was out with his Yeomanry, posed as their Mentor, that they learnt much about it. His lordship telegraphed to Elvaston for his ponies, mounted several would-be players, and taught them the elements of polo. The first match they played was against a team brought by Mr. Sydney Platt from Llanfairfechan, and commenced rather disastrously. Those were the days when charging for the ball was in vogue, and, on play commencing, Mr. Lane, who headed the charge for Chester, collided with Mr.

Platt, with the result that the latter and his pony were knocked over, the rider being rendered unconscious for a short period. They also played against the Manchester Club ; and one of their matches at Vale Royal, the seat of Lord Delamere, on the occasion of a great fête, is talked of to this day by the country folk as a great event.

The Roodee at Chester, that public resort which, besides being the Yeomanry training ground, racecourse, football, cricket, and hockey field, was then, as it is now, the arena on which poloists disported themselves, and it was no unusual sight then to see an un-trained pony, after a charge, " take charge " of its rider and carry him round the race-course before being induced to come into the game again. For some years the Club led a parlous existence, and polo died out at Chester, except during the Yeomanry week, when Lord Harrington kept things going. Matters are now, however, on a better foot-ing, as last year Mr. Tyrer revived the Club, and began by applying to the Chester Town Council for permission to level the ground. This was readily granted, and at a comparatively small cost he succeeded in making it a first-rate ground. Composed of sound old turf, it is 320 yards long and 160 yards wide—a great galloping ground, but of necessity not boarded. Mr. Tyrer's efforts to re-form the Club met with signal success, for it now numbers about twenty-eight playing members, whilst the Committee consists of Mr. A. D. Chambers, Mr. W. K. Court, Capt. W. Higson (late 4th Hussars), and Mr. J. H. Stock, M.P. ; whilst Mr. Eric Platt acts as hon. treasurer, and Mr. A. Tyrer, Plas Newton, Chester, is hon. secretary. Amongst the list of members will be found such well-known names as Mr. Blain, Mr. S. M. Dennis, Capt. T. M. Gordon (12th Lancers), Captain Higson, Mr. G. H. Pilkington, Sir Humphrey de Trafford, Mr. E. Tinsley, Mr. J. H. Stock, M.P., &c. ; whilst amongst promising men coming on may be mentioned Mr. George Wyndham, M P., and Mr. Moseley Leigh.

Much, however, as the Club owes its new lease of life to Mr. Tyrer, it owes more to the generous way in which they have been met by the Town Council of Chester, and especially to the courtesy of Mr. Enfield Taylor, the engineer to the Racecourse Company, for he has thrown himself heart and soul into the task of assisting them, and has afforded great facilities by lending the Club rollers and other machinery, and by giving them a place to keep their mowing machines, &c., besides the loan of dressing-rooms in the Grand Stand.

In such happy circumstances, and with a keen polo spirit springing up in the county, it is not too much to hope that the Chester Club may some day take back to the old city the Hurlingham County Cup, for which they made such a good fight in 1894. But they were, perhaps, consoled for their defeat by winning the Rugby Tournament after one of the best weeks of polo ever seen. They have the raw material; they are animated by keenness; and only want organisation and *practising together as a team* to make them a powerful combination.

THE WOLDINGHAM CLUB. — This, like many another Club, originated spontaneously in 1891. In that year Messrs. R. de Clermont, C. Taylor, F. S. Bristowe, F. A.

Edwards, H. Wilton, and one or two other
business men, were discussing the game
whilst travelling by train, and the outcome
of their conversation was that they determined to start the Club. Without a ground
and without ponies the matter was one of no
little difficulty, but they meant to succeed
and did so. A rough meadow was obtained
at Godstone, and the difficulty about ponies
was overcome by arrangements being made
with Mr. E. Woodland to have the Club, or
rather to find ponies on the hire system,
and a beginning was made. The next year
the ground was moved to Coulsdon, and
this was such an improvement that the
members of the Club got more and more
bitten with the game and determined to do
even better, and so towards the end of the
year a suitable ground was rented at Woldingham. The Club now became fairly
established; men bought ponies, a pavilion
was built and stabling erected for sixteen
ponies, whilst this was supplemented by Mr.
Walpole Greenwell kindly affording aid in
the matter of stabling at Marden Park.
The ground is a very fair one, 250 yards

long and 180 wide, and there is an excellent train service from town to Oxted, Redhill or Caterham, all of which are within easy reach of the ground. The Club numbers some forty-five players, a good many of whom put in an appearance on playing days, which are generally Wednesdays and Saturdays.

Though the Woldingham Club have not gone far afield to earn laurels, they have yet for such a young Club shown promising form, and have played Stansted, Woolwich Garrison, and a few other Clubs with satisfactory results. They *mean* to perfect themselves, and with this point in their favour will, no doubt, in time win their way to the front rank.

CHAPTER V.

Polo Clubs in the World.

N the September number (1894) of that amusing quarterly sporting magazine, *Fores' Sporting Notes and Sketches*, I came across an article by "Triviator" on "The Production of Polo Ponies," in which the writer seemed to me to have a slap at the game. He did indeed begin with the alliterative description of a "princely pastime," and brought to bear on his subject his whole artillery of classical quotations, and the result was a very readable article; but when he thus delivered himself I must confess that my hackles rose, and I growled as viciously as ever did an ill-tempered hound. Listen to him, polo players, and you who are interested in the breeding of the animal on which you are dependent for your fun, and say, had I not good reason, for thus our friend "Trivy" writes (see pp. 219-20) :—"If polo was certain. . . . animal than Fritz."

"Already there are signs of some waning in the interest taken in polo"! Are there? Let the answer be the following list—by no means complete, I fear—of the various Polo Clubs in the world. And when it is taken into consideration that a decade ago not a quarter of these existed, I think our "Trivy" is answered. And remember, please, that these do not include *Regimental* Clubs, that most cavalry regiments, both British and Indian, possess one, and that I have in a previous chapter enumerated the infantry regiments that play polo. Let me, therefore, submit the following list for your consideration, premising it by saying that I give it in alphabetical order and not with any idea of seniority or priority.

EUROPE.

ENGLAND.

Aldershot, Divisional.

Barton, J. R. Walker, Esq., The Knoll, Barton-under-
Needwood.

Berkshire.

Bowden, Harry E. Gaddum, Esq., Bowden, Cheshire.

Cambridge University, W. S Buckmaster, Esq.

Chester, A. Tyrer, Esq., Plas Newton, Chester.

Cirencester.

Derbyshire, Earl of Harrington, Elvaston Castle,
Derby.

Fetcham Park, A. Moon, Esq., Fetcham Rectory,
Leatherhead.

Grantham, Blundell Williams, Esq., Stamford.

Hurlingham, Captain Walter Smythe, Polo Manager,
Hurlingham Club, Fulham, S.W.

Liverpool, W. Lee Pilkington, Esq , Huyton Grange,
near Liverpool.

Ludlow, T. McMicking, Esq., Burway, Ludlow,
Salop.

Manchester, Douglas Phillips, Esq., The Cottage,
Chelford.

Monmouthshire, R. W. Kennard, Esq., Llwyn Du,
Abergavenny.

Oxford University, Viscount Villiers, New College,
Oxford.

Ranelagh, Rev. F. Dale, Polo Manager, Ranelagh
Club, Barn Elms, S.W.

Rugby, E. D. Miller, Esq., Spring Hill, Rugby.

Staffordshire, Earl of Shrewsbury and Talbot,
Ingestre Hall, Stafford.

Stansted, Tresham Gilbey, Esq., The Grange,
Bishop Stortford.

Sussex, A. Peat, Esq., South Hayes, Wimbledon.

Swindon, Dr. Toomer, Fair View, Swindon.

Tiverton, J. de las Casas, Esq., Collipriest, Tiverton.

Warwickshire, P. A. Leaf, Esq., The Brewery, Leamington.

Wellington, A. C. C. Kenyon Fuller, Esq., Finchampstead, Berks.

West Essex, Major Tait, Epping.

Wirral, F. W. Blain, Esq., Ashfield, Bromborough, Birkenhead.

Woldingham, P. M. Cleremont, Esq., Godstone, Kent.

Worcestershire.

SCOTLAND.

Edinburgh, T. B. Dryborough, Esq., 23, Grosvenor Street, Edinburgh.

IRELAND.

All Ireland, Captain Wood, Dishelstown, Castleknock, co. Dublin.

Antrim, Captain Ivan Richardson, Glenburn, Dunmurry, co. Antrim.

Carlow, Stewart Duckett, Esq., Russellstown Park, Carlow.

Fermanagh, T. E. T. Packenham, Esq., Enniskillen.

Freebooters, John Watson, Esq., Bective House, Navan, co. Meath.

Kildare, Colonel de Robeck, Gavan Grange, Naas, co. Kildare.

Londonderry, Andrew Watt, Esq., Londonderry.

Meath, Dr. Sullivan, Meath.

Sligo, R. St. G. Robinson, Esq., Sligo.

Tredeagh (Drogheda).

10

Westmeath, Captain E. Dease, Earlstown, Goole, Westmeath.

FRANCE.

Deauville.

Paris, M. Kellaire, Pelouse de Bagatelle, Paris. Hon. sec., M. R. Raoul-Duval, Marolles, par Genillé, Indre-et-Loire.

GIBRALTAR.

Gibraltar, O. W. Thynne, Esq., King's Royal Rifles, Gibraltar.

MALTA.

Malta

ASIA.

INDIA.

Polo Association of India, hon. sec., Major Sherston. Rifle Brigade.

Allahabad, Ahmedabad, Bangalore, Bannu, Barrack-pur, Bombay Gymkhana, Calcutta, Fort Sande-man, Hyderabad (Deccan), Jhansi.

Jhodpore, Major Beatson, Jhodpore.

Jubbulpore, Kirkee, Kirkee Gymkhana, Karachi, Lucknow, Madras Government House, Madras Gymkhana, Meerut, Mhow, Mian Mir, Ootaca-mund, Naini Tal, Nusseerabad, Peshawar, Poona Gymkhana, Quetta, Ranikhet, Roorkee, Saugor, Sealkote, Secunderabad, Umballa, Viceroy's Staff.

ASSAM.

Dibrugarh, A. M. Harry, Esq., Dibrugarh.

Jhanzie, F. Perman, Esq, Jhanzie Tea Estate, *via* Jorehât.

Jorehât, C. Miller, Esq., Cinneenara, Jorehât.

Lahwal, F. W Collins, Esq., Bokal, Dibrugarh.
Moran, Secretary, Moran Tea Estate, Sibsagor.
Nazira, J. Hulbert, Esq., Nazira, P.O. Sibsagor.
North Lakhimpur, Secretary, Joyhing.
Nowgong, Secretary, Nowgong.
Nudwa Road, G. W. Sutton, Esq., Dikom, Dibrugarh.
Panitola, A. W. Madden, Esq., Panitola, Dibrugarh.
Rishnauth, Secretary, Rishnauth Estate, Teypur.
Singlo, Secretary, Singlo Tea Estate, Sibsagor.
Teypur, Secretary, Teypur.
Upper Sudiya, F. E. Winsland, Esq., Tippuk, Dibrugarh.

BURMAH.

Bhamo, Kindat, Mandalay, Maulmain, Meiktila, Moniya, Mugwe, Rangoon, Myingyan, Pokoko, Shewbo, Thayetmo, Toungoo, Yamethin.

AFRICA.

Cairo, Dargle, Estcourt, Greytown, Government House, Mooi River, Rand (Transvaal).
Wanderers (Transvaal), Joseph Paterson, Esq., P.O. Box 647, Johannesburg, Transvaal.

AMERICA.

CANADA AND BRITISH COLUMBIA.

Beaver Creek, M. J. Holland, Esq., Beaver Creek Ranche, Alberta, N.W.T.
Calgary, Cannington.
Fort Macleod, E. A. Browning, Esq., Alberta N.W.T., Canada.
High River, Orlando (Florida).
Pincher Creek, E. M. Wilmot, Esq., Pincher Creek, Macleod, Canada.
Qu'Appelle River, Regina, Victoria (B.C.).

UNITED STATES.

U S. Polo Association, E. C. Potter, Esq., 36, Wall Street, New York.

Country Club of Brookline, F. Blackwood Fay, Esq., Brookline, Mass.

Country Club of St. Louis, John F. Shepley, Esq., St. Louis, Mass.

Country Club of Westchester, E. C. Potter, Esq., Westchester, New York.

Dedham, Samuel D. Warren, Esq., Dedham, Mass.

Devon (Philadelphia).

Essex County, T. H. P. Farr, Esq., Orange, New Jersey.

Harvard, C. C Baldwin, Esq., Cambridge, Mass.

Hingham, G. D. Braman, Esq., Hingham, Mass.

Meadow Brook, Oliver W. Bird, Esq., Westbury Long Island, N.Y.

Morris County, Benjamin Nicoll, Esq., Morristown, New Jersey.

Monmouth County, P. F. Collier, Esq., Hollywood, N.J.

Myopia, R. L. Agassiz, Esq., Hamilton, Mass.

Oyster Bay, F. T. Underhill, Esq , Oyster Bay, Long Island, N.Y.

Philadelphia, Charles E. Mather, Esq., Philadelphia, Pa.

Rockaway, John E. Cowdin, Esq., Cedarhurst, Long Island, N.Y.

Tuxedo, Richard Mortimer, Esq., Tuxedo Park, N.Y.

Westchester, Thomas Hitchcock, Esq., Newport, Rhode Island.

SOUTH AMERICA (ARGENTINA).

Association of the River Plate, F. J. Balfour, 559, Piedad.

Belgrano, J K. Cassels, Lavalle 108, Belgrano.

Bellaco, M. M. C. Henderson, Paysandu

Camp of Uruguay, L. Edwards, Barrancas Coloradas, Colonia.

Canada de Gomez, J. S. Robinson, C. de Gomez, F.C C A.

Casuals, R. McC. Smyth, Venado Tuerto.

Gualeguay, H. J. Perrett, Gualeguay, Entre Rios.

Hurlingham, F. J. Balfour, 559, Piedad, Buenos Aires.

Jujuy, H. Wright Poore, care of Leach Hnos y Ca., Salta, Argentina.

La Colina, O G Hoare, Santa Rosa, La Colina.

La Merced, P. H. Cawardine, La Merced, Chascomus.

La Victoria, Magnus Fea, Estacion, El Trebol, F.C. Central Argentino.

Las Petacas, Frank E Kinchant, Las Petacas, San Jorge, F.C.C.A.

Lezama, E. J. Craig, Estancia Las Barrancas, Lezama.

Medie Luna, Scott Moncrieff, Soler, F. C. Pacifico.

Montevideo, Fred A Christie, Club Inglés, Montevideo.

North Santa Fé, H. J. J. Bury, Las Limpias, Estacion Carlos Pellegrini, F.C.C.A.

Roldan, W. Ellery, Roldan, F.C.C.A.

Rosario, W. F. Christie, F.C.C.A., Rosario.

San Jorge, C. H. Hall, San Jorge, Estacion Molles, F C.C. del Uruguay, Montevideo.

Santa Fé, Kemball Cook, Las Tres Lagunas, Las Rosas, F.C.C.A.

Santiago del Estero, Dr. Newman Smith, La Banda, Santiago del Estero.

Tuyu, H. Gibson, Los Ingleses, Ajo, F C S

Venado Tuerto, H. Miles, Venado Tuerto, F.C.S. Santa Fé y Cordoba.

AUSTRALIA.

Adelaide, E. Laughton, Esq., jun.

Argyle, Ballarat, Brisbane, Broken Hill, Burra-Caramut, Camperdown, Coolak, Cooma, Dubbo, Goulbourn, Hamilton, Ipswich, Melbourne, Muswellbrook, Mount Crawford, Oaklands, Queanbeyan, Quirindi, Scone.

Sydney, Capt. A. J. Dodds, Australian Club, Sydney, N. S. Wales.

Wagga-Wagga, Werribee.

SAMOA.

Apia, T. B. Cusack-Smith, Esq., British Consulate, Apia.

NEW ZEALAND.

Auckland, Christchurch, Canterbury.

Elmwood, R. Heaton Rhodes, Esq., Christchurch.

Hobart Town, Kihi-Kihi, North Canterbury, Poverty Bay, Rangiora, Rangitiki, Wanganui, Weikiri.

In Jamaica I believe they play, and that there are one if not more Clubs in existence, but many letters having failed to elicit any reply from that land of sugar and "sangaree," I can give no details.

Now let us tot up the list, and we may, I think, add to it H.M.S. "Curacoa," for the sporting officers of that ship have earned a name for themselves as polo players, and take their ponies about with them on board, landing where they can on southern shores, and holding their own with any team that they have a chance of meeting. Sailors were ever sportsmen, but the names of these should be " clogged up in great gowd letters"! But to our addition sum. Giving Jamaica the credit of one club, and including H.M.S. "Curacoa," I make the number of Polo Clubs, not including Regimental Clubs, at over 200! This does not look as if there were signs of waning in the interest taken in polo !

One word in conclusion, addressed to polo players all over the world, where I hope this little book of mine will penetrate. I ask you to tell me of your Clubs, to give me particulars of them, their members and their ponies, their play and all matters connected with them, in order that, to the best of my ability, I may forge another link in the chain of polo history. The game *is* going ahead, no matter what its detractors may say. Let you and I assist each other mutually to hand down to posterity those who have helped on the grandest *game* there is, the one that must appeal most to the riding Briton—*POLO.* Long may it flourish !

CHAPTER VI.

The Hurlingham Club.

LAWS AND BYE-LAWS OF POLO, 1894

Rules and Regulations.

(1) *Height.*—The height of the ponies must not exceed 14 hands, and no ponies showing vice are to be allowed in the game.

(2) *Ground.*—The goals to be not less than 250 yards apart, and each goal to be 8 yards wide.

A full-sized ground should be 300 yards long, by 200 yards wide.

(3) *Size of balls.*—The size of the balls to be 3 inches in diameter.

(4) *Umpire.*—Each side shall nominate an Umpire, unless it be mutually agreed to play with one instead of two ; and his or their decisions shall be final.

Referee.—In important matches, in addition to the Umpires a Referee may be appointed, whose decision shall be final.

(5) *Number of players.*—In all matches for cups or prizes the number of players contending to be limited to four a side.

(6) *How game commences.*—The game commences by both sides taking up their position in the middle of

the ground, and the Manager throwing the ball in the centre of the ground.

(7) *Duration of play.*—The duration of play in a match shall be one hour, divided into three periods of twenty minutes, with an interval of five minutes between each period of play.

The two first periods of play shall terminate as soon as the ball goes out of play after the expiration of the prescribed time ; any excess of time in either of the first two periods, due to the ball remaining in play, being deducted from the succeeding periods. The last period of play shall terminate immediately on the expiration of the hour's play, although the ball is still in play.

Exception —In case of a tie, the last period shall be prolonged till the ball goes out of play.

(8) *Changing ponies*—As soon as the ball goes out of play, after the expiration of the first ten minutes of each period of play, the game shall be suspended for sufficient time, not exceeding two minutes, to enable players to change ponies. With the above exception, play shall be continuous, and it shall be the duty of the Umpire to throw in the ball punctually, and in the event of unnecessary delay in hitting out the ball, to call upon the offending side to proceed at once. Any change of ponies, except according to the above provision, shall be at the risk of the player.

(9) *Bell.*—A bell shall be rung to signify the time for changing ponies, and at the termination of each period of play.

(10)—An official Time-keeper shall be employed in all important matches.

(11) *Tie.*—In all tournaments, the game, in case of a tie, after an interval of five minutes, must be played on till one side obtains a goal.

(12) *Goals.*—A goal is gained when a ball is driven between the goal posts, and clear of the goal line, by any of the players or their ponies.

(13) *Over top of goal posts.*—If a ball is hit above the top of the goal posts, but in the opinion of the Umpire, through, it shall be deemed a goal.

(14) *To win game.*—The side that makes most goals wins the game.

(15) *Where ball to hit from position of players.*—If the ball be hit behind the back line by one of the opposite side, it shall be hit off by one of the side whose line it is, from a spot as near as possible to where it crossed the line. None of the attacking side shall be within 30 yards of the back line until the ball is hit off. If, however, the ball be hit behind the back line by one of the players whose line it is, they shall hit it off as near as possible to where it crossed the line, and all the defending side shall remain behind the line until the ball is hit off, the attacking side being free to place themselves as they choose.

(16) *Ball thrown in by Umpire.*—When the ball is hit out of bounds, it must be thrown into the ground by the Umpire from the exact spot where it went out of play, in a direction parallel to the two goal lines, and between the opposing ranks of players.

No delay allowed.—There must be no delay whatsoever, or any consideration for absent players.

(17) *Riding out an antagonist.*—A player may ride out an antagonist, or interpose his pony before his antagonist, so as to prevent the latter reaching the ball, but he may not cross another player in possession of the ball, except at such a distance that the said player shall not be compelled to check his pony to avoid a collision.

Definition of crossing.—If two players are riding from

different directions to hit the ball, and a collision appears probable, then the player in possession of the ball (that is, who last hit the ball, or if neither have hit the ball, the player who is coming from the direction from which the ball was last hit) must be given way to.

(18) *Crooking stick.*—No player shall crook his adversary's stick, unless he is on the same side of the adversary's pony as the ball, or in a direct line behind.

(19) *Off side.*—No player who is off side shall hit the ball, or shall in any way prevent the opposite side from reaching or hitting the ball.

Definition of off side.—A player is off side when at the time of the ball being hit he has no one of the opposite side between him and the adversaries' goal line, or behind an imaginary line drawn parallel to the goal line, and he is neither in possession of the ball nor behind one of his own side who is in possession of the ball. The goal line means the eight yard line between the goal posts or that line produced. The position of the players is to be considered at the time the ball was last hit, *i.e.*, a player if on side when the ball was last hit, remains on side until it is hit again.

(20) *Rough play.*—No player shall seize with the hand, strike, or push with the head, hand, or arm below the elbow.

(21) *Carrying ball.*—A player may not carry the ball. In the event of the ball lodging upon or against a player or pony, it must be immediately dropped on the ground by the player or the rider of the pony.

(22) *Penalty for foul.*—Any infringement of the rules constitutes a foul. In case of an infringement of Rules 17, 18, 20, and 21, the Umpire shall stop the game ; and in case of an infringement of Rule 19, the Umpire

shall stop the game on an appeal by any one of the side which has been fouled. On the game being stopped as above, the side which has been fouled may claim either of the following penalties.

(*a*) A free hit from where the ball was when the foul took place, none of the opposing side to be within 10 yards of the ball.

(*b*) That the side which caused the foul, take the ball back and hit it off from behind their own goal line.

(23) *Penalty for disabling a player.*—In the case of a player being disabled by a foul, the side who has been fouled shall have a right to designate any one of the players on the opposite side who shall retire from the game. The game shall be continued with three players aside, and if the side that causes the foul refuse to continue the game, it shall thereby lose the match. This penalty shall be in addition to that provided by Rule 15.

(24) *Changing ends.*—Ends shall be changed after every goal, or if no goal have been obtained, after half-time.

(25) *Ball out.*—The ball must go over and clear of the line to be out.

(26) *Throwing in ball.*—If the ball be damaged, the Umpire must at once stop the game, and throw in a new ball at the place where it was broken, and at right angles to the length of the ground, and between the opposing ranks of players.

(27) *Broken sticks.*—Should a player's stick be broken, he must ride to the place where sticks are kept and take one. On no account is a stick to be brought to him.

(28) *Dropped stick.*—In the event of a stick being dropped, the player must pick it up himself. No dismounted player is allowed to hit the ball.

(29) *Ground kept clear* —No person allowed within the arena—players, umpires, and Manager excepted.

(30) *Accidents.*—That in the event of any player having a fall, or if, in the opinion of the Umpire, any player shall be hurt in any way to prevent his playing, the Umpire shall in that case stop the game and allow time for the dismounted man to mount, or the injured man to be replaced.

(31) *Where ball thrown in.*—On play being recommenced, the ball shall be thrown in, where it was, when the accident occurred.

(32) *Disregarding Umpire's decision.*—Any deliberate disregard of the injunctions of the Umpire shall involve the disqualification of the team so offending.

(33) *Umpire's power to decide all disputes.*—Should any incident or question arise that is not provided for in these Rules, such incident or question to be decided by the Umpire.

BYE-LAWS

(1) *Officers selected to serve on Polo Committee.*—Every Regiment having amongst its officers four Members of the Hurlingham Club, starting a team in the Inter-Regimental Polo Tournament, and which is not already represented, shall have a right to elect one Officer (being a Polo player and a Member of Hurlingham) as a Member of the Hurlingham Polo Committee; and this Officer shall be a Member of the Committee for one year from the time he is elected.

(2) *Time shortened.*—In order that all members may play during the afternoon, the Manager shall have power to shorten the time, and stop the Match or game at the appointed hour. If a Match is timed to commence at 4, 5.20 shall be the time at which it may be stopped.

(3) *Time.*—On ordinary days, in cases of a match taking place before the members' game, such match must finish at 5, unless by special leave from the Committee. This does not apply to the tie games in Cup Competitions.

(4) *Registration.*—All Polo Clubs must be registered with the Manager on May 15th in each year. A Book of Rules and Members of such Club to be forwarded at time of registration.

(5) *Ponies property of Club, &c.*—In matches for cups or prizes the ponies must be *bonâ fide* the property of the Club or Regiment contending.

(6) *Spurs and blinkers.*—No blinkers, or spurs with rowels allowed, except on special occasions when sanctioned by the Committee

(7) *Measurement.*—Each pony to be passed under the 14 hand standard by the Manager and two of the Polo Committee. A book to be kept by the Manager, in which the height of all ponies belonging to members is to be entered A pony five years old or aged, after having been passed, is not required to go under the standard again.

(8) *Four players.*—Not more than four players on each side are allowed to play.

Precedence.—The members arriving first at the Pavilion to be allowed precedence

(9) *Whistle.*—The Umpire shall be required to carry a whistle, which he shall use as required

(10) *Time of ground being opened and shut.*—If, in the opinion of the Manager, the ground is in a fit state for play, it shall be opened for not less than six players, at 3 o'clock each day, Fridays excepted, when the ground is closed Each set of players shall be allowed the use of the ground for 20 minutes. All play shall cease and the ground shall be cleared by 7.15 p m.

(11) *Colours.*—The colours of the Hurlingham Club shall be light blue shirts. The second colours white and red sash. In members' matches every player shall wear a white shirt or jersey, the sides being distinguished by red and blue sashes, supplied by the Manager.

CONDITIONS FOR THE COUNTY CLUB CUP.

OPEN TO ALL REGISTERED CLUBS.

(1) *Conditions.*—Any Member playing for his Club must be a resident in the County where such Club has its ground, or reside within 50 miles of the Club Ground.

(2) *Three years.*—No member of a Team who has played for the Open Cup and won the same during the last three years is eligible to contend.

(3) *University.*—Oxford and Cambridge University Clubs can play.

(4) *Residence.*—A residence within the metropolitan area of London cannot act as a qualification for a Middlesex or Surrey Club.

(5) *Entries.*—Entries to be made in writing to the Manager at least ten days previous to the date fixed for the first game, giving the names and addresses of each player.

(6) *Five pounds lodged.*—The Captain of each Team on entering to deposit Five Pounds with the Manager, which shall be returned on the Tournament concluding.

Should the Team be scratched the Five Pounds shall be forfeited and go to the Team which is second.

(7).—The number of players on each side is limited to four.

(8) *Substitution of player in case of accident.*—In the event of one of the players being prevented from playing from some *bonâ fide* good reason, the Polo Committee may, if they think fit, allow another man, properly qualified, to be nominated in his place ; such substitute must not, however, be taken from among the players selected in any other Team.

CONDITIONS FOR CUP TOURNAMENTS.
CHAMPION CUP CONDITIONS.

(1) *Open.*—Open to all registered Polo Clubs and Regiments.

(2).—The number of players on each side is limited to four.

(3) *Entry form.*—The entries, naming colours, to be made on or before 5 p.m., on the Saturday prior to the week of competition.

(4) *Draw.*—The respective Teams to be drawn, and the said draw to take place on Saturday, at 5 p.m., prior to the week of competition.

Name players.—The Captain of each Team to name his four players at time of entry.

(5) *Substitutes.*—In the event of one of the players being prevented from playing from some *bonâ fide* good reason, the Polo Committee may, if they think fit, allow another man to be nominated in his place; such substitute must not, however, be taken from among the players selected in any other Team.

(6) *Three teams.*—Unless three Teams contend the Cup will not be given.

(7) *Tie.*—In case of a Tie between two Teams, it must be played off the same day till one Team obtain a Goal, always excepting both Teams elect to postpone.

CHAPTER VII.

RULES OF THE INDIAN POLO ASSOCIATION.

RULES FOR THE REGULATION OF TOURNAMENTS, &c.

(1) *Maximum height of ponies.*—The new rules for the measurement of ponies shall have effect from April 1, 1893. The maximum height of polo ponies shall be thirteen hands and three inches.

(2) *Stewards.*—All tournaments played under the rules of the Indian Polo Association shall be under the management of three stewards, who shall be elected locally.

(3) *Right of appeal to stewards.*—There shall be a right of appeal to the stewards upon all questions which are not by these rules declared to be subject to the final decision of some other authority, such as umpires, &c., and the decision of the stewards in all such appeals shall be final.

(4) *Questions to be referred to stewards.*—Any question which may arise in the course of a tournament and which is not provided for by these rules, shall be referred for decision to the stewards, who may, if they think fit, refer the matter to a committee of five members of the Indian Polo Association, whose decision shall be final.

11

(5) *Limit of time and number of ponies.*—The duration of play, and the number of ponies allowed to be played by teams in a tournament, shall be decided by the local stewards of each tournament : provided that the maximum duration of play in any match does not exceed forty minutes, exclusive of stoppages.

(6) *Annual meeting.* — There shall be an annual meeting of Members of the Indian Polo Association during the Inter-Regimental Tournament. No alteration in the rules, or constitution of the Indian Polo Association, to be made except at this meeting ; due notice having been given to all members by the honorary secretary.

(7) *Existing tournament polo ponies.* — All ponies registered by the Indian Polo Association on or previous to April 1, 1893, in accordance with the rules in force prior to that date, as having played in a recognised tournament previous to March 31, 1892, shall be entitled to life certificates.

(8) *Aged ponies.*—Ponies over six years old, when once measured by the independent authority to be appointed, and in accordance with the rules to be laid down by the Indian Polo Association, may be given life certificates by the Association. Racing certificates will not be accepted.

(9) *Rules for measurement.*—The stewards of every tournament shall nominate a committee, consisting of three members, to measure all ponies not holding life ertificates which are intended to be played in a tournament. No pony shall play in a tournament unless—

    (*a*) It has got a life certificate.

    (*b*) It has been measured and passed by the committee Such committee to assemble at the station where the tournament is held, within one week of such tournament. The honorary secretaries of tournaments will advertise in a daily newspaper published in the province in which the place is situated, the date of assembly of such committee. Not less than seven days' notice shall be given

(10) The inspection of ponies shall take place during the week previous to the commencement of the tournament.

(11) Ponies may be aged or measured by the stewards of the Indian Polo Association, and by the persons duly authorized for that purpose by such stewards. Ponies shall be aged and measured at such times and places only as the stewards of the Indian Polo Association shall determine.

(12) Any two of the persons, empowered under Rule 11, shall form a quorum for the purpose stated ; and if more than two act the decision shall be that of the majority.

(13) *Rules for measurement.*—If, after the publication of the notice referred to in Rule 9, the necessary quorum cannot be obtained owing to the inability of any person to attend or act, the stewards of the Indian Polo Association may appoint a substitute for such person.

(14) No person shall take any part in ageing or measuring his own pony or a pony in which he has an interest.

(15) The person presenting a pony to be aged or measured shall fill up and sign a form containing such particulars as the stewards of the Indian Polo Association shall from time to time direct. The following shall be the form :—

OWNER	COLOUR	CLASS.	SEX	NAME	REMARKS

Signature

Date

Place

(16) When the age or height of a pony is determined, the name, colour, and distinguishing marks of such pony, as well as his age and height, shall be entered in a register kept for the purpose ; and the entry as regards such pony shall be signed by all the persons who have taken part in the determination. If the entry is made in a register which is not kept by the Secretary of the Indian Polo Association, the sheet containing it shall be forwarded to the said Secretary without delay, and shall be filed in the office of the Indian Polo Association.

(17) Any person who is dissatisfied with the determination arrived at may, by written application presented within three days, apply for another determination. A note of the application shall be made in the register referred to in Rule 16 ; and if the pony is presented at a time and place of which due notice shall be given, he shall be again aged or measured, as the case may be. The particulars of the second determination shall be entered in the register above-mentioned, and the determination shall be final If the pony is not presented at the time and place fixed, the original determination shall hold good, unless the stewards of the Indian Polo Association direct otherwise.

(18) A pony shall not be measured if he appears to have been subject to any improper treatment with a view to reduce his height, or if he is in an unfit state to be measured, and he shall not be aged or measured if he is unnamed, or if all the particulars required under Rule 16 are not furnished. If a pony is rejected on the ground that he has been subjected to improper treatment, the persons before whom he is brought may order that he shall not be again presented within a period of six months.

(19) For every pony presented to be aged or measured, there shall be paid in advance a fee of Rs. 2. Such fee shall be credited to the Indian Polo Association.

(20) Any person may, on payment of a fee of R. 1, obtain from the secretary of the Indian Polo Association a certified extract of an entry in the register referred to in Rule 16

(21) The following rules shall be observed in measuring ponies :—

(1.) The pony shall stand stripped on a perfectly

level platform, and the measurement shall be made at the highest point of the withers with a measuring rod of a pattern approved by the stewards of the Indian Polo Association.

(ii) He shall be held by a person deputed by the persons conducting the measurement, and he shall not be touched by any one else without their permission.

(iii) The head shall be so held that a line from the poll to the wither would be parallel to the platform

(iv.) The forelegs from the point of the shoulder, and the hind legs from the back downwards, shall be as perpendicular to the platform and and as parallel to each other as the conformation of the horse allows

(v.) The wither may be shaved, but the mane must not be pulled down, or the skin of the neck or wither in any way interfered with.

(vi.) No allowance shall be made for shoes.

(vii) Not more than five minutes shall be allowed for the measurement.

(22) In ageing ponies a veterinary surgeon shall, if possible, be consulted.

(23) In case of the number of entries for any tournament not being a power of 2, as 4, 8, 16, &c., all byes shall be in the first round. For instance, 13 teams enter, 3 draw byes, the remainder play off, leaving 8 to play in the second round.

(24) Each team to consist of not more than four players.

(25) Native teams may be admitted as honorary members of the Indian Polo Association without voting powers.

(26) All Station, Regimental, and Battery Polo

Clubs can become members of the Indian Polo Association on payment of a donation of Rs. 5.

RULES OF THE GAME.

(1) *Duration of each match.*—Each match shall last for not more than forty minutes exclusive of stoppages and intervals. Time shall not be called while the ball is in play, unless the game shall have lasted forty minutes, when time shall be called, irrespective of the ball being in play.

(2) *Time.*—Time may be called whenever the ball is out of play, and the game shall be stopped for two minutes, at the expiration of which the umpires must call play.

(3) *Ties.*—In the event of a tie the goal flags shall be placed forty-four feet apart, and the game shall be immediately started as directed in Rule 18.

Play to continue for eight minutes, when time shall be called, unless the game is still a tie, in which case play shall be continued until one side gets a goal.

(4) No team shall be compelled to play on two consecutive days, except in the case of a tie.

(5) *Interval.*—Three minutes' interval shall be allowed after every period, it being optional, if both sides agree, to have no interval; but three minutes must not be exceeded.

(6) *Umpires.*—The stewards shall nominate two umpires and four goal referees for each match. Those selected as umpires must be regular Polo players, and must possess a thorough knowledge of the game.

(7) *Powers of umpires to order players off the ground.*—The umpires shall have the power of ordering off the ground any player who, after having been warned,

plays unfairly or rides dangerously, and it shall be his duty to do so. Such player shall not be replaced.

(8) Each umpire shall be provided with a whistle, the blowing of which by either umpire is a sign that the game is to stop till the decision is given.

(9) *Power of umpires to order dangerous ponies off the ground.*—The umpires shall order off the ground any pony which they may consider dangerous or improperly bitted, or which the rider has not under thorough control.

(9*a*) In order to be able to discharge their duties properly, umpires must be mounted on well-trained and fast ponies, so as to be able to ride near enough to the ball to give a decision at any moment, and yet not to interfere with the players.

(10) *Power of umpires to order play to begin.*—The umpires shall have the power of ordering play to begin after the time fixed, notwithstanding the absence of any player.

(10*a*) In the event of an accident, the umpires are empowered to stop the game.

(11) *Decision of umpires final.*—The decision of the umpires shall be final on all questions declared by these rules to be subject to their final decision, and shall also be final on all questions arising out of the actual play of the game, except on questions arising out of Rules 36 and 37, on which questions the umpires shall have no voice.

(12) *Decision of "goal referee" final.*—The decision of the "goal referee" standing at the goal in question, shall be final as to whether the ball has passed between the goal flags or subsidiary goal marks.

(13) *Size of ground.*—The size of the ground shall be as nearly as possible 300 yards long and 200 broad, and shall be marked off by flags.

(14) *Goals*.—At each end of the ground, in the centre of the back line, there shall be a goal marked by flags which shall be 22 feet apart. The line between the goal posts shall be called the goal line.

(15) *Sides to toss for choice of goals.*—Sides shall toss for choice of goals.

(16) *Change of goals.*—Goals shall be changed after every goal obtained. Should the game continue for two periods without a goal being obtained, goals shall be changed ; but should any goal afterwards be obtained, goals shall be changed after that goal, and after any subsequent goal, without reference to time.

(17) *Size and weight of balls.*—The ball shall be of bamboo root, about ten and a half inches in circumference, and four ounces in weight.

(18) *The starting of the game.*—To start the game and after each goal, the ball shall be thrown into the centre of the ground by one of the umpires dismounted, the two sides ranging themselves opposite each other, the ball always to be thrown in from the same side of the ground.

(19) *When ball becomes dead, and course to be then followed.*—The ball on being hit out at the side line, shall be thrown in under hand, as soon as possible, by one of the umpires, or by any one deputed by him to do so, in a straight line at right angles to the line and as hard as possible—the ball to touch the ground before passing the side line. The ball shall be considered to be in play as soon as it crosses the side line, unless the umpire should immediately call it back. The umpire shall be the sole judge as to whether the ball is properly thrown in or not. The thrower is to be on foot.

(20) *Course to be followed when ball hit behind back line* (1) *by one of opposite side.*—If the ball is hit behind the

adversary's back line by one of the opposite side, it shall be hit off, by one of the side whose line it is, from a spot as near as possible to that at which it crossed the line. None of the opposite side shall stand within thirty yards of the line until the ball is hit off.

(21) (2) *By one of side whose line it is.*—If the ball is hit behind the back line by one of the side whose line it is, it shall be hit off from the nearest corner by one of the opposite side ; no other player of that side shall stand within thirty yards of the back line until the ball is hit off, and all the players of the side behind whose back line the ball is being hit, shall stand behind their own back line.

The above rule shall be enforced at the option of the side who have the right to hit off from the nearest corner. If they decline to enforce this rule, the ball shall be hit off according to Rule 20, excepting that the side from whose back line the ball is being hit off shall stand behind their own back line.

(22) *Hit off.*—The ball shall be considered to have been hit off when it has been hit across the back line with the intention of hitting off.

(23) *Small flags to be placed.*—Small flags shall be placed on the side lines to mark fifty yards and thirty yards from the back line, and a section of a circle shall be marked off at each corner of the ground with the corner for the centre and a radius of five yards.

(24) *No unnecessary delay to take place in reviving the ball.*—No unnecessary delay shall take place in reviving the ball under Rules 19, 20 and 21. Any necessary delay shall not count as actual play.

(25) *No player to cross or ride dangerously.*—No player shall cross or ride dangerously.

(26) *Course to be followed when two players are in danger*

of collision, when coming from opposite directions —If two
players are riding to hit the ball from different directions, and a collision appears probable, the player
not in possession of the ball must give way to the
player in possession of the ball. The player who hit
the ball last, or who has come in the same direction
as the ball did when last hit, is in possession of the
ball.

(27) *No person other than umpires and players to come
on ground.*—No person other than the umpires and
players shall come on the ground while the ball is
in play

(28) *In " riding off " or " hustling " no player to make
use of his arm below elbow.*—" Riding off " is permitted.
" Hustling " is not. The penalty for hustling shall be
the same as that for dangerous riding.

The following is a general definition of " riding
off "

(28*a*) *Definition of " riding off."*—(*a*) A player shall
be considered to " ride off " fairly, when having
placed himself abreast of an adversary (after following a line of direction as nearly as possible parallel
to that in which his adversary is moving) he gradually
forces him from, or prevents his continuing in, the
direction in which he is riding. This definition to be
considered together with Rule 25 " on crossing."

(*b*) In so " riding off " a player shall be permitted
to use his arm between the shoulder and the elbow,
provided the elbow be kept close to the side.

(*c*) Any other attempt to ride off shall be hustling.

(*d*) Players must not play left-handed,

(29) *Course to be followed when a player catches the
ball.*—If any player catch the ball in any way during
the game, it must be dropped on the ground at once

(30) *When a player may crook an adversary's stick* —

Subject to the next rule, a player may crook, or stop an adversary's stick, when the adversary is about to strike the ball.

(31) *Players not to place stick over, across or under adversary's pony.*—No player shall at any time place his own stick over, across or under the body of an adversary's pony. No player shall crook his adversary's stick unless he is on the same side of the adversary's pony as the ball, or immediately behind.

(32) *No player to interfere when "off-side."*—No player, when "off-side," shall be allowed to hit the ball, or in any way interfere in the game, intentionally or otherwise; should he do so the penalty of foul can be claimed.

(33) *Definition of "off-side."*—A player is "off-side" when, at the time of the ball being hit, he has no one of the opposite side between him and the adversary's goal, and he is neither in possession of the ball nor backing up one of his own side. He shall be deemed to remain " off-side ' until he shall have passed by one of his own side who is " on-side," or until the ball shall have been struck or struck at by an adversary, provided that such adversary shall be between him and the adversary's goal.

(34) *Player not to take part in game while dismounted.*—No dismounted player shall be allowed in any way to take part in the game while dismounted.

(35) *" Broken ball."*—If in the opinion of the umpire the ball is sufficiently damaged to interfere with the game, he shall stop the game, and a new ball shall be thrown in from the side nearest to where the ball was broken and at right angles to it, the players ranging themselves in the same way as when the ball is out of bounds.

(36) *How a goal may be obtained.*—A goal is obtained

if the ball be hit between the flag-posts of the goal; or if it be kicked by a pony between the flag-posts of the goal; or if being hit higher than the top of the posts it would, in the opinion of the goal referee, have gone between the posts produced; or if it be hit over the goal line between the two points where the goal posts should stand, when either or both the goal posts shall have been displaced. The ball must go over and clear of the line to count as a goal.

(37) A subsidiary goal is obtained in the same way as a true goal, except that to score a subsidiary goal, the ball must pass between the subsidiary goal mark and the goal post which is nearest to it.

Subsidiary goal.—The subsidiary goal marks must be shown on the ground by a white line, and not by flags.

Subsidiary goals are to be measured eleven feet from each goal post on the outside—the sum of the subsidiary goal thus equals the true goal. No number of subsidiary goals will ever equal a true goal. In the event of a tie in the actual number of goals, the side scoring the greater number of subsidiary goals will be considered the winner.

(38) *Goals not to count when obtained by unfair play.*— No goals or subsidiary goals shall be counted which have been obtained by unfair play.

(39) *What is " unfair play " or " a foul."* — Any infringement of the rules constitutes " unfair play " or " a foul."

(40) *Penalty in case of " foul" being declared* —In case of " a foul," other than crossing or dangerous riding, being declared, the umpire shall stop the game, and either of the two following penalties may be claimed by the side which has been declared to have been fouled :—

(*a*) A free hit from where the ball was, when the "foul" occurred, and none of the opposite side to be within ten yards of the ball. But if the "foul" occurs near the goal of the side which causes the "foul," a free hit shall be given from a spot not within thirteen yards of the goal, but as near as possible to where the "foul" occurred.

(*b*) That the side which caused the "foul" take the ball back and hit it off from behind their own back line, and they shall stand behind their back line until the ball is hit off.

(41) *Penalty for crossing or dangerous riding.*—The following shall be the penalty for crossing or dangerous riding.—In the event of a "foul" being given for crossing or dangerous riding, the following shall be the penalty. A free hit from a spot fifty yards from the back line of the side causing the "foul" and as nearly as possible opposite the spot where the "foul" took place, unless the "foul" takes place less than fifty yards from the back line, in which case the free hit shall be given from the spot where the "foul" occurred; all the side causing the "foul" to be behind the back line until the ball is hit off, but not between the goal posts.

CHAPTER VIII.

TOURNAMENTS AND WINNERS.

THE following is a list of some of the principal Tournaments and the winners since the date of their inauguration.

HURLINGHAM OPEN CHAMPION CUP.

Date	Winners
1877.	Monmouthshire Club.
1878.	Monmouthshire Club.
1879.	Hurlingham Club.
1880.	Sussex County Club.
1881.	Sussex County Club.
1882.	Sussex County Club.
1883.	Sussex County Club (walked over).
1884.	Freebooters.
1885.	Sussex County Club.
1886.	Freebooters.
1887.	Freebooters.
1888.	Sussex County Club.
1889.	Sussex County Club (walked over).
1890.	Sussex County Club.
1891.	Sussex County Club.
1892.	Sussex County Club.
1893.	Sussex County Club (walked over, but did not take the Cup).
1894.	Freebooters.

HURLINGHAM INTER-REGIMENTAL TOURNAMENT.

Date	Winners.
1878.	5th Lancers.
1879.	5th Lancers.
1880.	16th Lancers.
1881.	16th Lancers.
1882.	5th Lancers.
1883.	7th Hussars.
1884.	7th Hussars.
1885.	7th Hussars.
1886.	7th Hussars.
1887.	5th Lancers.
1888.	10th Hussars.
1889.	9th Lancers.
1890.	9th Lancers.
1891.	9th Lancers.
1892.	13th Hussars.
1893.	10th Hussars.
1894.	13th Hussars.

HURLINGHAM INFANTRY TOURNAMENT.[1]

1890.	5th Northumberland Fusiliers.
1891.	5th Northumberland Fusiliers.

HURLINGHAM COUNTY CUP.

1885.	Gloucestershire Club.
1886.	Gloucestershire Club.
1887.	Derbyshire County Club (walked over).
1888.	Kent County Club.
1889.	Barton-under-Needwood Club.
1890.	Berkshire County Club.
1891.	Liverpool Club.
1892.	County Meath Club.
1893.	Edinburgh Club.
1894.	Edinburgh Club.

---

[1] This tournament has since been discontinued.

ALL IRELAND OPEN CUP.

Date	Winners.
1878.	7th Royal Fusiliers.
1879.	7th Hussars.
1880.	Scots Greys.
1881.	5th Lancers.
1882.	All Ireland Polo Club
1883.	County Carlow Club.
1884.	5th Lancers.
1885.	Freebooters.
1886.	Freebooters.
1887	All Ireland Polo Club.
1888.	All Ireland Polo Club.
1889.	Freebooters.
1890.	All Ireland Polo Club.
1891.	13th Hussars.
1892.	9th Lancers.
1893.	13th Hussars.
1894.	15th Hussars.

THE ALL IRELAND REGIMENTAL CHALLENGE CUP.

1886.	10th Hussars.
1887.	16th Lancers.
1888.	3rd Hussars.
1889.	4th Hussars.
1890.	4th Hussars.
1891.	15th Hussars.
1892.	13th Hussars.
1893.	9th Lancers.
1894.	10th Hussars.

PARIS INTERNATIONAL TOURNAMENT

1893.	17th Lancers.
1894.	Hurlingham Club.

12

Indian Inter-Regimental Tournament.

Date.	Winners
1877.	9th Lancers.
1878.	9th Lancers.
1879	No tournament in these years owing to the
1880.	Afghan war.
1881.	10th Hussars.
1882.	10th Hussars.
1883.	9th Lancers.
1884.	9th Lancers.
1885.	9th Lancers.
1886.	8th Hussars.
1887.	8th Hussars.
1888.	17th Lancers.
1889.	17th Lancers.
1890.	5th Lancers.
1891.	7th Hussars.
1892.	Queen's Bays.
1893.	Queen's Bays.
1894.	Queen's Bays.

The Malta Tournament.

1889.	49th (Berkshire) Rgt.
1890.	49th (Berkshire) Rgt.
1891.	41st (Welsh) Rgt.
1892.	49th (Berkshire) Rgt.
1893.	41st (Welsh) Rgt.
1894.	2nd (Queen's) Rgt.

Indian Native Cavalry Cup.

1890.	9th Bengal Lancers.
1891.	9th Bengal Lancers.
1892.	14th Bengal Lancers.
1893.	9th Bengal Lancers
1894.	14th Bengal Lancers.

INDIAN INFANTRY TOURNAMENT.

Date	Winners.
1890.	18th (Royal Irish) Rgt.
1891.	14th (West Yorkshire) Rgt.
1892.	61st (Gloucester) Rgt.
1893.	61st (Gloucester) Rgt.
1894.	2nd Batt. Durham Lt. Infantry.

PUNJAUB TOURNAMENT.

1886.	12th Bengal Cavalry.
1887.	12th Bengal Cavalry
1888.	12th Bengal Cavalry.
1889.	12th Bengal Cavalry.
1890.	12th Bengal Cavalry.
1891.	Patiola
1892.	Patiola.
1893.	Patiola

APPENDIX.

The Polo Pony Stud Book Society.

It may be interesting, in connection with this handbook on Polo, to give a short account of the Polo Pony Stud Book Society, in which the late Mr. Moray Brown took such a deep interest. The Society is the outcome of many meetings and much correspondence in the *Field, Live Stock Journal, Land and Water,* and other papers on the subject of pony breeding. A great want was felt of such a Society and of a stud book, but opinions were so varied and interests so conflicting, that the whole scheme was nearly being entirely lost. However, eventually, upon a meeting being called by Mr. John Hill, of Felhampton Court, to be held during the show of the Royal Agricultural Society at Chester, on June 20th, 1893, all former

disagreements were loyally forgotten ; Mr.
Moray Brown brought all his great personal
influence and knowledge of the subject to
bear, and the present Society was on that
day formed on such a sound basis that in
less than two years its success and popularity
are established. As the preface to the first
volume of the Stud Book states — " The
Society was formed for the registration of
all ponies suitable for *riding* purposes, and
for the production of such ; the ' weight-
carrying ' blood polo pony being the type
which the Society considers the one to be
aimed at. At present there is no distinct
breed of ' riding ' ponies, and there is no
animal scarcer or worth more money as a
pony than one which will carry a heavy man
safely and easily as a hack—a pony standing
from 14 to 14.2 hands, with bloodlike head,
intelligent eye, well set on neck, shoulders
strong, but sloping well into the back, good
deep barrel, well coupled loins, tail well
carried, long quarters, clean cut hocks, and
hard wear and tear forelegs. Made something on such lines as these, he must be a
safe and fast walker, putting his feet down

without catching his toes, and stepping well out from the shoulder. Such a mover almost invariably can trot, canter, and gallop as a matter of course. High trotting action is not required, in fact, is an objection in most cases when breeding 'riding' ponies, in distinction to those of the harness type."

The above quotation will show the objects of the Society, which accepts ponies of all heights not exceeding 14 hands 2 in., but none are admitted without being inspected by one of the judges appointed by the Council. By this inspection rule it is hoped to lay the foundation of the future breed of riding and polo ponies on as firm ground as possible. The first Council consisted of twenty-four members, with the Earl of Harrington as its President. This number has now been increased to thirty, the President for 1895 being Sir Humphrey de Trafford, and Mr. Fredk. Wrench, of the Irish Land Commission, has again been elected as Vice-President. The influential support, both from polo players and pony breeders, is most encouraging; but the irreparable loss the Society has sustained by the

the death of its warmest patron, Mr. Moray Brown, is indeed a heavy one. It is hoped, however, that his many friends will rally round the cause he had so sincerely at heart, and use every effort to make it the success which he was working so hard to secure. One of his latest actions in connection with it was, on behalf of the Ranelagh Club, to invite the Society to hold its first show of ponies on its ground, and he was instrumental in fixing the very best day in the year for the date, viz., the Wednesday following the Derby, June 5.

By holding an annual show, and by supplementing the prizes given by other Societies, or by awarding medals on the same principle as that which has been adopted by the Hunter Improvement Society, the breeding of high-class riding and polo ponies may be greatly encouraged. The impetus already given to the business has been considerable, many studs having been formed, while the owners of old established strains recognise an increasing value to their property from the fact of their being able to record the pedigrees in the Stud Book. It is, perhaps, worth while to mention that the United States Government has already acknowledged the Society, and will permit the importation of any animals for breeding purposes free of duty, if they are accompanied with certificates issued by the Society for the purpose. Several animals have been exported under these favourable conditions. The name and address of the Secretary of the Society are Mr. Fredk. R. Hill, Felhampton Court, Church Stretton.

INDEX.

—

13

Milton Keynes UK
Ingram Content Group UK Ltd.
UKHW022103040823
426370UK00005B/109